Transition to Teaching:

by
Linda L. Bain and Janice C. Wendt,
University of Houston

Sponsored by the
National Association for
Sport and Physical Education

an association of

AAHPERD

The American Alliance for
Health, Physical Education,
Recreation and Dance

A Guide for the Beginning Teacher

Purposes of the American Alliance For Health, Physical Education, Recreation and Dance

The American Alliance is an educational organization, structured for the purposes of supporting, encouraging, and providing assistance to member groups and their personnel throughout the nation as they seek to initiate, develop, and conduct programs in health, leisure, and movement-related activities for the enrichment of human life.

Alliance objectives include:

1. Professional growth and development—to support, encourage, and provide guidance in the development and conduct of programs in health, leisure, and movement-related activities which are based on the needs, interests, and inherent capacities of the individual in today's society.

2. Communication—to facilitate public and professional understanding and appreciation of the importance and value of health, leisure, and movement-related activities as they contribute toward human well-being.

3. Research—to encourage and facilitate research which will enrich the depth and scope of health, leisure, and movement-related activities; and to disseminate the findings to the profession and other interested and concerned publics.

4. Standards and guidelines—to further the continuous development and evaluation of standards within the profession for personnel and programs in health, leisure, and movement-related activities.

5. Public affairs—to coordinate and administer a planned program of professional, public, and governmental relations that will improve education in areas of health, leisure, and movement-related activities.

6. To conduct such other activities as shall be approved by the Board of Governors and the Alliance Assembly, provided that the Alliance shall not engage in any activity which would be inconsistent with the status of an educational and charitable organization as defined in Section 501(c) (3) of the Internal Revenue Code of 1954 or any successor provision thereto, and none of the said purposes shall at any time be deemed or construed to be purposes other than the public benefit purposes and objectives consistent with such educational and charitable status.

Bylaws, Article III

Table of Contents

Preface

Teacher education programs attempt to prepare prospective teachers for the responsibilities of teaching by developing the preservice teachers' skills and knowledge and by using field experiences as a laboratory for applying these abilities. However, beginning teachers frequently experience problems in the transition from the university to the "real world." Confronted with the challenges of this work arena, the beginning teacher must negotiate this novel territory and develop patterns of behavior which will produce a satisfying professional career. The success of this initial adjustment to teaching is essential to the implementation of quality physical education programs and to the teacher's own career satisfaction.

The National Association for Sport and Physical Education recognized the importance of this transition to teaching and initiated this publication. The goals of the project were developed by the NASPE College and University Physical Education Council and the Secondary School Physical Education Council. Valuable input was received from members of both groups, but the authors accept sole responsibility for the content of the book. Gratitude is expressed to Dot Kirkpatrick and Ronald Carlson for their reviews of the manuscript and helpful suggestions. A special thanks to Donny Fort for his contribution of illustrations.

1

Starting off on the Right Track: an Overview

So the time has come. You've finally arrived. Student teaching or that new job is at hand. You were assigned to just where you wanted to be, or maybe you're terrified to be at the school you were assigned. Possibly you got that job you always wanted; maybe even yet, you feel lucky to have a job at all. Even though you've completed all that tedious coursework and processed and signed all that paperwork, the worst and best is probably yet to come. You begin the year with a set of mixed emotions. Excitement is high, yet concern is great. Will I know enough? Will the students like me? Will other teachers respect me? Yes, the challenge of this new career is great. All of these feelings are natural. It's okay to be nervous, and you probably will make a few mistakes. What you're dealing with in teaching is often your reaction to a set of complicated, quickly occurring set of events. The school district itself is an active, dynamic social arena, reacting to subjective reasoning which is constantly being stimulated by various issues. In becoming oriented to a new school, you have to consider the social and political atmosphere as well as the impact it will have upon your interactions and job.

The initial orientation you will receive will vary from school to school. Let's face it, you may or may not receive the help you need to get your feet on solid ground, so you will need to help yourself. Table 1 at the end of the chapter provides a checklist for you to use in obtaining the answers as your new assignment is begun. It is important to start off on the right foot for a smooth transition from student to teacher. If you start your teaching experience at the beginning of a school year, it will probably be somewhat easier than starting off in the middle of the term. Why? Both the teacher and students are starting off together in this new venture at the onset of a new school year. But, the teacher is still "in charge" of the class and can exercise some degree of control over the situation regardless of when it begins. The length of time required to gain total control will, of course, vary both with the groups of students with which you work and with your ability to bring the class to a desired level of manageability.

So—where to begin? First, look at yourself. Review your purpose for being in the teaching profession in the first place. Why did you want to be a teacher? What is important to you as a teacher? What do you hope to accomplish? How do you view children? Examine your feelings toward the challenge of teaching. The strength of a commitment often begins with personal honesty. Don't just play

1

a role. If you don't have strong feelings about teaching and wanting to teach, it may be more difficult for you from the start because teaching is a very demanding and physically fatiguing profession. Identify the basic values of the teaching profession and consider how you feel about each. Certainly the welfare of others and public service must be at or near the top of the list. No? Possibly not for you, but the public, the school board, students, parents, and administrators alike expect, yes, *expect* this to be an important part of your commitment to teaching. What about a commitment to helping in the growth of the student? Do you view students as obstacles to your success? Do you view your teaching as a battle against ignorance? These views are often in conflict with helping the student learn. You must teach from a positive position that will lead to the growth of your students. How you feel about teaching is as important as your professional preparation. Schools work toward responsible citizenship, sound family relationships, and worthy use of leisure time. You must have and maintain positive feelings about teaching these values for you to accomplish these important goals of education. What? What about money, power, and prestige? You can find a great deal of self-worth and satisfaction in teaching if you are identified with the goals of education; however, if you have strong needs for money, power, and prestige, you must accept the teaching profession's definition of these factors. This definition varies from the business world where wealth, power, and status are measured in terms of materialistic personal gain. You probably won't get monetarily rich in the teaching profession. The successful teacher will have the wealth of seeing students advance and succeed in life. It's a large paycheck when a former student states, "I owe it to my teacher who helped me believe in myself." When examining finances, check out the salary scale at the school district, and see where you'll be ten years from now. This will give you some perspective for the long-term monetary benefits of teaching. It is extremely important to do some introspective thought as to why you're in teaching and what your true feelings are about those goals. If these values are unresolved in you, look closely at the self-awareness exercises in Chapter 5.

Now that you've looked at yourself and examined your goals, look at the expectations of the community and administration. One of your first goals will have to be fitting into and becoming a part of the community and school. It's too early to attempt to change the system. You must first examine the terrain. Is the community and school traditional? Do you see many good innovations already incorporated in the structure of the school? Are the learning aids traditional or of a timely nature? Do the equipment and facilities reflect any interest or emphasis in your area of expertise or the subject matter which you plan to teach? Look at the course offerings, student handbook, or faculty handbook for clues indicating the overall philosophy of the school. The school's perception of the community's values should be reflected in these materials. If you perceive that the community and school are traditional in nature and philosophy, this is a clear indication that any change attempted will proceed very, very slowly with administrative approval before each change can be accepted. The change you're interested in may be as simple as introducing a new activity into the school's curriculum. Don't follow through without specific approval from your supervisor. If you're interested in being innovative, be sure to consult "Initiating Change" in Chapter 3. It is important to remember that if you are not one who likes to maintain the status quo, you may experience problems in staying in a traditional school even though you may know how to work the system. Remember, tradition is often the way people in the community like things done.

Get a clear picture of the principal's philosophy toward education, discipline, control, etc. Hopefully, you already have some ideas resulting from your initial interview or meeting with the teachers, or you have a friend who works for the district. Do not count only on the principal, department chairperson, teachers, or whoever to orient you. It is your responsibility to orient yourself. Be critical of the information you are given. Be cautious when considering early discussions with other teachers about administrators. Students don't have a monopoly on the "tattle-tale" syndrome, and you can be "burned" or embarrassed to say the least. Some teachers have administrative aspirations and will make disclosures for administrative recognition. Remember, there are many fine teachers who will do all they can to help you; just be careful in whom you choose to confide. Review, study, and become knowledgeable of the policies and procedures of the school district. Be alert to watch for the "gap between the way things are supposed to be and the way they are." Generally, when a crisis over values or procedures occurs, the formal structure will probably prevail. Choose friends carefully. If you have a friend who teaches or has taught in the district and you feel you can level with him/her, try to get an idea of what is expected of you concerning duties, discipline, etc. Ask your friend to be a good critic who would assist you in keeping your job with the school district. Find out how much balancing between conformity and innovation may take place. What is the tension level within the school? Is it high, low, or does it vary with the present issue? How will your idealism be received? Don't become personally transparent to the employees or students too soon by being overly verbal about your feelings, fears, insecurities, and apprehensions. Find out the security status of the campus as well as the administrators' philosophy toward this issue.

Do some detective work. Try to gain knowledge of the informal structure of the school. Who's considered a good teacher, a good disciplinarian, who's related to whom, who is in what clique, and who are the "yes" persons or informants to the principal. The informal social structure in certain situations may be more powerful than the formal. Your success in teaching may depend on the accuracy of your perceptions of what is accepted as "good" and where the power lies.

During those somewhat informal days before school begins or time before you begin your student teaching, be sure and attend the inservice programs (usually provided at the beginning of the year) which will give you valuable information and help you get started. You might obtain some good information on how to deal with problems or where to go if you do encounter a problem. Don't be a recluse. Talk with other teachers. Ask their advice. Listen to other teachers talk about school administration and students.

Begin to form an accurate picture in your mind about the informal structure of the school. Most experienced teachers appreciate and like being asked for their suggestions on how to deal with certain issues. Think ahead. Attempt as much as possible to pose the problem "what if?" rather than wait until something has happened and having to ask, "what do I do?" Select your friends wisely and tune in to sound advice.

Look at the student and faculty handbooks again and study them intensely. Look carefully at the policies and procedures listed for students and teachers.

Make sure the rules you establish do not conflict with those of the school and be certain that the disciplinary measures for infractions are consistent with school policy. Become aware if your department has policies which cover attendance and the behavior of students in class. See if fellow teachers have a list of rules of expected behavior which are given to the class. Design and utilize a set of rules and/or guidelines which will clearly reflect your expectations for the students. Also be sure that both you and the students can and do abide by them.

Find out what the policy is and procedures are when disciplinary problems are not responsive to teacher-administered disciplinary action. Ascertain what kinds of disciplinary action is taken by the administrator as well as what the administrator thinks about teachers who send their discipline problems to him/her. Try to handle your disciplinary problems as often as you can so that minor issues aren't paraded to the principal's office. A good administration should back you and let you know where you stand.

Overplan for the first week's activities. Know what facilities are available for you to use and when. Ascertain the people and programs using the physical education indoor and outdoor facilities and if there is a coordinating person or calendar. Anticipate interruptions and irregularities the first few weeks of school. If you care about your subject matter, these interruptions can make class a frustrating experience. If outdoor activities are planned, have an alternate indoor plan. Above all, make sure the equipment and/or facilities are available for use. Alternate facilities, equipment, and/or activities may need to be considered. Never be totally dependent on equipment, technology, films, facilities, etc. In any instance, plan ahead for unstructured time for students in case facilities, equipment, etc. become unavailable. Quite often students must be taught how to constructively utilize unstructured time. This freedom can occur later on in the semester when you have a good "grip" on the class.

Teacher peer pressure can also be a potential problem. Some teachers and school principals may attempt to put pressure on the new teacher to join organizations or pet projects of their choosing. Attempt to get all the facts about the groups before you attempt to become a part of the group. Being inexperienced creates many apprehensions in the new teacher. Often the first concern of this teacher is to survive the teaching situation at all cost. That usually means a combination of not letting the students get out of hand and being respected as a competent colleague. That is a tall order. Concentrate on the reality of what you are, not just projecting the "proper" image to colleagues.

Since you're still somewhat uncertain as to your respect from other colleagues, you must make a concerted effort to fit in with the group. Genuine respect is earned over a period of time. As a new teacher, you must "prove" yourself without being a threat to the other professionals. Yes, you are a professional now! You won't accomplish too much by trying to change things overnight and you might threaten some potential beneficial relationships. *Go slowly* before you attempt change. Good rapport must be established with the experienced teacher if you hope to become a part of the team. Probably more teachers choose to leave a school setting because of relationship problems with administrators, teachers, and/or students than for any other reason. Some teachers can be just as vicious as students when they are threatened. The time for major changes in curriculum or whatever occurs later on when you have become accepted by your peers and the administration. They will probably be more willing to hear and accept what you say and do then. Being organized, having prior information, being nonthreatening and maintaining a high energy level is a tall order for the new teacher. This can be accomplished!

Table 1. Orientation guide to the new teaching experience.*

I. **General Information.**
  A. Demographical Data.
      1. School system:
      2. Complete school name:
      3. Personnel director for school system:
      4. If appropriate:
         dean of students:
         guidance counselor(s):
         department chairperson:
         athletic director:
            boys:
            girls:
         school nurse:
         head custodian:
      5. Superintendent:
      6. Principal:
      7. Vice-assistant
         principal(s):
      8. School board:
         president:
         members:
  B. Teacher Requirement Data.
      1. Time teachers report to school?
      2. Time teachers can leave school?
      3. Are teachers required to sign in and out of school? Where?
      4. Procedures teachers follow if sick or absent?
      5. Will I be required to perform special duties such as hall, lunch, or bus duty?
      6. What are the requirements for teachers relative to faculty mtgs., department mtgs., or extracurricular activities such as Athletics, P.T.A., or open-house functions?
  C. School Policy/Organization/Services Data.
      1. What is the general chain-of-command procedure to follow in discipline situations?
      2. Are there special policies to follow for chronic absentees?
      3. What are the procedures to report absentees in classes?
      4. Are there special procedures to follow for tardy students?
      5. Are hall passes or permission slips used? How?
      6. Are "homerooms" scheduled in class day? When?
      7. What procedures are to be followed to arrange observations of other faculty in physical education and other classes?
      8. Will I be allowed to use instructional resources, media equipment, and copier equipment and are there special procedures to follow for these?
      9. What is the general socio-economic background of the students?
      10. What percentage of the students are transported to school by bus?
      11. Will I be given a student and faculty handbook and will there be a special orientation to the material within these handbooks? By whom?

*Adapted from materials developed by Ronald Carlson, Indiana University.

D. Health/Safety/Accident Data.
1. Is a school nurse on duty?
   Time: Days: Location:
2. What forms/procedures do I use if a student is injured in class?
3. Will I be instructed on plans for emergency evacuations?
   a. Fire drill procedure from gym/teaching station (procedure written up?).
   b. Disaster procedure from gym/teaching station (procedure written up?).
   (What are my specific responsibilities in the above situations?)
4. What types of daily/weekly excuses are accepted and how are they authorized?
5. What procedures are normally followed when a student returns to class following an extended absence (injury or illness)?
6. Are there special resources for teachers to check out specific health/participation restrictions of students?
7. Are there parental permission slips sent home with students that state specific policy and safety rules to be acknowledged by both parents and the student for certain activities such as gymnastics, swimming, or track and field?
8. Ask yourself these questions:
   a. Did I check out all safety hazards in the teaching area to be used?
   b. Did I inform my class thoroughly of these hazards and related rules?
   c. Did I bring to the attention of school authorities possible hazards in my teaching area (in writing and retaining a copy)?

II. Physical Education Class Data.

A. Policy/Procedures/Organization.
1. Is there a departmental handbook for teachers to follow?
2. Is there a student policy/procedure sheet for students?
3. Is there a course of study (curricular guide/yearly curriculum schedule) available?
4. What type of attire are teachers required to wear during the teaching of classes?
5. What, if any, are the requirements for student dress in activity classes? Is this requirement used as part of their grade?
6. Pre-class phase/procedures.
   a. How are locks/lockers assigned?
   b. How are lost locks, equipment, and personal items handled?
   c. Are there special locker room procedures to follow? Supervision by whom?
   d. What is the roll call procedure used? Does it change with specific activities?
   e. Is there an opportunity for general pre-class activity before the instructional phase begins? Type of activity?
   f. Are classes started with the traditional exercise period? Or is there a special procedure for certain activities?
   g. Is a special check-out system procedure used to disperse equipment for both the teacher and student?
   h. What procedure do I follow to procure equipment for my units of instruction?
7. How are squads and/or teams designated? (Who makes up squads/teams?)
8. What activities are taught as coed classes?
   a. Boys' classes only?
   b. Girls' classes only?
9. Will I teach as one member of a team-teaching approach? What activity? Duties?

10. What is the grading system used by the department? What are the areas of evaluated behaviors? Skills? Knowledges? Conduct? What is the weighting of these areas? How are grades reported to class? What code/symbol is used (P/F)? What options/limitations will I be given in grading my units of teaching? When are reporting periods? Are progress reports given out?

B. Staffing/Curriculum/Special Data.
1. Will I be required to assist in extracurricular activities?
2. Will there be any inservice days for the department faculty? When? Where? What is the topic?
3. Are atypical students mainstreamed into all classes or just in a special activity or activities? (Find what limitations exist of those students mainstreamed into the class.)
4. Are special adapted (intact) classes scheduled separately for atypical students?
5. Will special education teachers assist in mainstreamed classes?
6. Are there any special handling procedures to use for atypical students?
7. What units of activity will I be exposed to during my experience and what units will I teach myself?
8. What type of daily lesson plan and unit plan formats am I expected to use? Are they to be examined? If so when and to whom are they given?
9. Will I have available or be expected to use an instructional bulletin board?
10. Will I be expected or will I be permitted to generate instructional study guide hand-outs?
11. What professional education organizations does the school recommend I join when I begin to teach?

III. Athletic Responsibilities.

A. Pre-season.
1. Finalize my schedule and send a copy to all opponents. Obtain phone numbers, addresses, and schedules from all opponents. The state school directory will be of great help.
2. Run a strong conditioning program (under supervision if allowed).
3. Determine the first possible practice date and schedule gym time accordingly.
4. Organize a league or city-wide coaches meeting. Discuss rules, tournament policies and procedures, and selection of officials if this hasn't been set.

B. In-season.
1. Eligibility requirements. Is there a minimum GPA for participation as well as continual participation? School requirements? Interscholastic league requirements?
2. Does the school charge an "athletic fee" for participation on a team? What happens when a student is put off the team?
3. Is the school going to provide practice suits or do the students provide their own?
4. Maintain a good working relationship with the athletic director and other coaches. Invite them to games.
5. Is there an attendance policy for practice and games?
6. Is a trainer available to be at practice and matches?
7. Can I have a team manager to assist with uniforms, prepare for home and away matches, etc.?
8. How is transportation arranged for away matches? What paperwork is needed and when is it to be filed? Do I have to serve as chauffeur? Who pays for a bus driver if one is used?
9. Will admission be charged for the home games? Does it go into a general fund? Who controls the use of the profits?

10. Who makes game-day preparations? Clocks, scoreboards, announcers, concession stands, ticket takers, officials, sweeping, and cleaning up afterward?

C. Off-season.
1. How are equipment and uniforms ordered?
2. When is the budget submitted for the following year?
3. Set up an off-season training program and/or practice if allowed and feasible (gym space available).
4. Can I recruit within the school or in the district schools that promote into the school?
5. Begin securing next year's schedule and reserve gym time.
6. Is there a Booster Club which supports my group?
7. Can I raise funds for my teams' use?

(Go back through I. D and II and answer those questions as they relate to the coaching assignment.)

2
Managing the Tasks: Handling the Daily Routine

The task is at hand. Soon the students will arrive. Those last-minute preparations and details you spent time on will help you immensely during this first week of stress and confusion. Remember, you're not the only one confused and frustrated; so are the students. They don't quite know what to expect either. They are just as concerned about your impression of them as you are of their impression of you. You will be involved in possibly as many as 1,000 interactions with students and/or peers on this day and every other day that you are in the teaching arena. What you say is important, but *how* you say it may even be more important. Understanding what is involved in being a leader and being assertive will help you to come across in a positive manner.

Being a Leader

A leader is a person who influences others. Leadership is directly concerned with people and their behavior. The definition, "the effort to influence or change the behavior of others in order to accomplish organizational, individual, or personal goals"[1] is characteristic of the role of the teacher in the schools. Generally, two types of leaders are present within the structure of the class: the formal leader; the informal leader. The formal leader is one who has legitimate power and authority over the group whereas the informal leader emerges because he/she has been able to influence the other members of the group in certain ways. Power is the ability to control one's environment. (See Chapter 3.) The teacher is the formal leader of the class. Keep a careful watch to discover who might be an informal leader of each class. There may be more than one in a class. This informal leader is generally a student who is either well-liked or presents a certain amount of expertise in an area that students admire. As a teacher you would do well to take advantage of this "leader" and use him/her to expose the other students to the kind of behavior you would like emulated in class. Classrooms experience numerous power struggles. Give the informal leader power at times, but don't let this person *take* it from you.

---

[1]Huse, E. F., and Bowditch, J. L. *Behavior in Organizations: a Systems Approach to Managing.* Reading, MA: Addison-Wesley, 1973, p. 145.

Traits which seem important in influencing others vary, but these characteristics appear most often: the ability to communicate and listen; a strong desire to achieve; being conscientious and self-confident; positive and sincere attitudes toward subordinates; enthusiasm.[2] It is important to remember that you can acquire any of these traits to complement your other good qualities. In addition to desirable qualities, certain behaviors on your part can make your task easier.

As a leader, you must set the example. Students look to you for appropriate behavior and direction. Don't be caught reinforcing inappropriate behavior unless you are willing for it to continue. As important as it is to "know yourself," it is equally important to know your students. The "hey, you!" approach is seldom effective except in alienating the student. One of your first goals should be to learn about your students. Know their names, their strengths and weaknesses, and use their talents accordingly to help you with the activities planned within the class. If you have students with expertise in soccer, utilize them in demonstrating skills and as peer teachers. Plan activities that will give you some insight into the nature and behavior of your students.

Spend some time in the first week trying to learn the students' names not only as a defense in coping with the complexities of teaching but in an effort to fit the name with the personality. Make up games or incorporate name tags, particularly for small children, which will aid you in learning your students' names as well as in controlling the group. Be aware that some students love to switch names and tags to further confuse the issue. Be willing to give a little in this situation if possible because other students might enter into the game and cause more confusion. A check of the high school student's driver's license might be the remedy, but don't make too much fuss over the issue. Also try not to rely too heavily on students for answers against their peers for peer pressure often forces the children to peer conformity.

A good leader is "we"- oriented, not "I"-oriented. Together you and your students should work toward certain goals within the structure of the class. Develop a sense of leadership responsibility in others. You can't do it all by yourself. Delegate responsibility as necessary within the structure of the class, and encourage the group to seek responsibility and to value accomplishment. The informal value structure must not overpower the class goals, or it should be capitalized on to benefit the class. For example, if class competition is great within your school, using a goal-setting technique can keep the class working together to accomplish a task. In a fitness unit the goal can be the total minutes improved for the entire class after successive trials in the mile run as compared with other classes. If class norms are aimed at "fun," build it into the reward structure for pulling together and accomplishing a task. Remember not every task within the class is appropriate for delegation to students. Having your students record absences or grade papers might put you and the students on a collision course with peer pressure as well as the administration.

As a leader, give recognition when deserved, and avoid correcting someone in front of others. Be tactful. Some people (students, teachers, and administrators alike) will defend their self-image in the eyes of their peers at all cost. Develop a sense of humor to see you through trying times, and become a

---

[2]Kossen, S. *The Human Side of Organizations*. San Francisco, CA: Canfield Press, 1978.

student of human nature. Admit when you are wrong, for false fronts seldom command respect. Avoid using authority to insulate your emotional insecurity. Authority is the last resort, not the first. Encourage constructive criticism, *but,* make sure you can handle it. You may also be guilty of defending your image at all cost. Take the responsibility for your actions. Don't "pass the buck" or make excuses. Know yourself and seek improvement. Be a stronger leader tomorrow than you are today. Anticipate difficult situations in advance. Make sound and timely decisions. It helps if the decision made is the right one. Consult specialists when complex problems are encountered, and draw from the experience of others.

Your leadership behavior goes back to those original questions about your philosophy toward teaching and how you view students. It's all interrelated. Your philosophy toward teaching will influence your approach to leadership. If you believe that your students are free spirits and need to have avenues for the expression of this "spirit," you will probably find that you tend to have activities which will vent this freedom of expression. However, if this approach tends to bring out chaos or carefree abandon, and you also value organization and control, your philosophy and leadership style may be on a collision course. Knowing this about yourself helps you to deal with the problem and allows you to plan other activities which will be more in line with your values.

Endorsing the positive philosophy of teaching to improve or enhance the growth of the student enables you to be more positive in your approach to leadership in the classroom. However, if you are negative in your approach to leadership, believing that students are by nature disinterested and unwilling to learn, or if you're battling ignorance, you might find you will spend more time "putting out fires" than constructively organizing, directing, and controlling. This approach can also be more frustrating, defeating, and less pleasurable as a way to live each day with your students. It's easy to get depressed if you stay negative too long. You tend to give fewer positive strokes and find it more difficult to show pleasure in students' behaviors.

Many guidelines have been given for the new leader. It is advisable that you reread the guidelines from time to time and reevaluate your leadership perspective, because different problems arise causing concern. It helps greatly to solve the problematic issues in which you find yourself involved.

Being Assertive

Assertiveness as well as nonassertiveness are actually learned patterns of responding in social situations.[3] When one thinks of assertive behavior, more often than not, adjectives such as aggressive, declarative, affirmative, demanding, or insisting are used to describe the quality. Whatever the definition, assertive individuals compel others to recognize and attend to their requests. How this comes about is a combination of what an individual says as well as *how* one says it. The attitude that is expressed in the assertive individual is that of a "winner" displaying all the confidence and self-assurance possible to handle the situation. The strength of your commitment to teaching should be all

---

[3]Rathus, S. A., and Nevid, J. S. *Behavior Therapy.* Garden City, NY: Doubleday and Doubleday, Inc. 1977.

the foundation that the dedicated teacher requires. However, if you don't think you are very assertive, you might want to take advantage of assertiveness training.[4]

Assertive behavior involves both verbal and nonverbal messages. It can be expressed directly by telling a student to come to attention or listen, or it can be expressed indirectly by moving close to the student, standing over him/her, maintaining strong eye contact, and giving a "sharp" look which indicates one is being asked to pay attention. Continue this posture until the desired behavior occurs, or respond verbally if necessary. Generally, nonverbal vehavior is a better way of handling a problem when dealing with students. Avoid the possibility that dual contradictory messages are being given. For instance, if you are standing over the student in a position of power and you are unhappy with the behavior and you smile and give pleasant supportive behavior, the student is confused as to which message he/she is to follow. You may also be the recipient of a mixed message from another teacher or administrator; sometimes it is difficult to detect which message to follow. The teacher who wants his/her students to be enthusiastic about a new activity cannot sit on the bleachers taking care of other business, i.e., grading papers or looking over coaching strategies, and still expect the students to love the activity in which they are involved. Your nonverbal behavior should support your verbal behavior.

Being assertive is not being irritable and lashing out at students. It is not being punitive or inconsistently pressuring students or faculty. It isn't being authoritarian because you have a desire for control and power. Assertive behavior of teachers in the eyes of the students should always be based on the principle of commitment to one's teachiing philosophy and the expectations of the district.

What does it take to be assertive? Be confident of your ability and speak in a confident manner. Students sense when you are unsure of yourself and often see this as a weakness in the new teacher. Often the new teacher attempts to maintain roll call or instruction while the students are talking and thus, not listening. What usually happens is the new teacher attempts to "outshout" the students to gain attention and control. Not only is this unassertive, but it does not handle the problems of the students demanding attention. Instead the assertive teacher must remain composed, firm, and bring the class to attention before continuing the activity. Maintaining eye contact generally shows confidence. Some weak teachers actually attempt to teach by never looking at their students and merely focus on the wall above their heads or look at their notes lifting their heads only when the bell rings. This relays to the students that their teacher is unsure, disinterested, or uncaring. It is difficult for a teacher to actually know what's going on in the class and possess that important quality known as "with-it-ness." This quality enables the teacher to have "eyes" in the back of his/her head and "antennae" which sense everything that is happening in the room. "With-it-ness" is significantly related to managerial success and is an important quality for effective teachers to possess.[5]

Being in a power position, e.g., standing while students are sitting, being in front of the class rather than in peripheral, unnoticed places, and being close to

---

[4]Ibid., 1977.

[5]Cooper, J.; Hansen, J.; Martorella, P.; Morine-Dershiner, G.; Sadker, D.; Sadker, M.; Shostak, R.; Sokolove, S.; Tenbrink, T.; and Weber, W. *Classroom Teaching Skills: a Handbook.* Lexington, MA: D. C. Heath and Co., 1977.

students rather than far-removed, places you in the position to be more assertive. Do not use approval-seeking behaviors, placating, pleading, or apologetic exchanges, if you hope to be assertive. You may be emitting a mixed message. Approval-seeking behaviors often indicate to the student that you do not feel in control of the situation. Be firm, be consistent, and be fair in your approach to students, and communicate the feeling that *you are a leader*.

Directing the Class

You may think that being in charge of a class of students is somewhat presumptuous. Actually it is closely akin to being on stage or in a competition and having the spectators judge your performance. In this situation (school), all the players (teachers and students alike) are subject to the same close scrutiny. Defensive behaviors as well as the desire to perform satisfactorily all emerge within the individual almost simultaneously as the tasks at hand are encountered. Will the students like me? Will I be able to control the class? Do I know enough to teach? Will the teacher like me? Can I perform the tasks adequately so that I won't be embarrassed in front of the students and/or teacher. All these questions and concerns are surfacing in the individual causing teachers and pupils alike to respond accordingly. Don't underestimate the individual's need, whether a student or teacher, to save face in front of a group. Don't reprimand or back a student into a corner without expecting some kind of defensive behavior on his/her part to save face in front of peers. As a teacher, you may find yourself in this same position with students, when they force you to defend yourself. Try to anticipate when this can happen and avoid taking a threatening, lashing-out posture against the students. Be careful for some students confuse professional ethics with personal weakness in the teacher.

An important contribution to the direction of the class is a set of rules which govern the behavior in the class. Write these rules in a positive manner. Instead of "Don't chew gum," write "Food, drinks, and gum are to be left out of the gymnasium." Make sure your students know the consequences of their behaviors, and above all provide a reward structure for when their behavior is good. Table 1 gives you some sample rules, consequences, and rewards. Try

---

Table 1. A discipline plan.

Rules
1. Food, drinks, and gum are to be left out of the gymnasium.
2. Wear proper attire before participating in the activity.
3. Abusive language must be avoided during class.
4. Students are to remain quiet while instruction is given.
5. Be safe and protective of classmates and equipment.

Consequences
1. Warning for expulsion.
2. Isolation for 10 minutes.
3. Sent to principal.

Rewards
1. Give recognition.
2. Five minutes of designated free time.
3. Choice of activity for one period.

Table 2. Write your own discipline plan!

Class rules. (Remember to state them in positive terms. Don't have too many.)

Consequences. (State in words that students understand.)

Rewards. (List what your students would enjoy that can be a reality.)

your hand at making rules, consequences, and rewards for your class in Table 2.

Be sure to discuss and give these rules to the students at the first class meeting, and include what happens in case of infractions. Each student should have a copy of these and even send a copy to the parents for verification, signature, and return. Have the student sign a form indicating his/her understanding of the rules so another game, "You Didn't Tell Me," or "I Didn't Know" won't be valid. Keep the students' and parents' signatures in an accessible place. Now that you have established rules, make sure you are consistent in their enforcement, or they are without meaning.

Make an attempt to understand what motivates the behavior of students. Dreikurs and Cassel's[6] approach to handling misbehavior takes a positive stance when working with students. They believe that by understanding the goals of the students' misbehavior, the teacher can act accordingly. The four common goals of misbehavior in students are: attention-seeking; power-seeking; revenge-seeking; displays of adequacy. Table 3 is provided for you to record other behaviors which you recognize that follow those goals.

The attention-seeker, for example, needs to be satisfied receiving the attention of the teacher or other students. Attention given the student for inappropriate behavior (punishment) may be more desirable to that student than no attention at all. The attention reinforces the behavior and causes that behavior to be repeated. Therefore, the kind of attention given by the teacher must be positive to reinforce the desired behaviors the teacher wants to see. By giving the student attention when he/she leads exercises in front of the class, demonstrates a new skill, helps with equipment, etc., the need is being reinforced in a positive manner. Continued needs for attention will diminish as this basic necessity is satisfied. The recommended reading list at the end of this

---
[6]Dreikurs, R., and Cassel, P. *Discipline without Tears.* New York: Hawthorne Books, 1972.

chapter is an excellent resource for helping you to frame your philosophy toward discipline.

Table 3. Goals of misbehavior.

Teacher Feels:	Student Behavior:	Student Goal:	Teacher Correction:
Annoyed	Shows-off Clowns	Attention	Ignore if possible. Give + attention.
Angry	Lies Argues Is disobedient Refuses work	Power	Withdraw conflict. Enlist cooperation.
Hurt	Physical attack Vicious	Revenge	Avoid punishing. Develop trust.
Despairing Helpless	Passive	Display of inadequacy	Stop all criticism. Encourage.

When dealing with interruptions or disruptive behavior in class, remain calm in handling the intrusion into the lesson. Interruptions can be in the form of students, public address systems, other teachers, or administrators. Have a plan of action to put into motion when this occurs. Work this out with the students before interruptions take place. Either make sure they know they are to continue the activity or spend a few quiet moments until you are once again available to continue class. Make sure they know what kind of behavior is improper. During the first week interruptions will probably be commonplace. Have the presence of mind to stay "cool" and keep the situation under control. If the interruptions are due to the behavior of a student within the class, the same plan of attack is valid. Handle the student preferably on a one-to-one basis to avoid any face-saving measures by the student. Make sure the students know what behavior you find acceptable and which other behaviors are unacceptable. The interrogative approach can be used to get at the problem with an individual student or with a class.

Having a Confrontation

Invariably an issue surfaces and the teacher is faced with a problem which can create a confrontation with a student. Confrontations can be constructive or destructive to those involved be it student or teacher. Constructive confrontations result in clarification of values, improved communication, accurate exposure and knowledge of issues, a sincere desire to follow up with the solution, improved cohesion of parties, and personal growth for the individuals involved. Conversely, destructive confrontations result in partial communication, supercharged emotion lacking logic and missing the issue, loss of respect, and alienation of the parties involved. Serious confrontations should not take place in front of the class for the need to defend one's image is too great and will invariably get in the way of the issue. Four guidelines should be kept in mind:

1. Stay on the subject.
2. Use the emotions involved to gain insight into additional problems.
3. Be sure that ideological disagreement is not confused with personal hostility.
4. Resolving the issue is more important than winning.

A good example of a confrontation not staying on the subject occurred when the teacher told the student, "Son, get off the bleachers!" The student replied, "I'm not your son!" to which the teacher retorted, "I wouldn't want you for my son!" This confrontation was also destructive in the relationship between the teacher and the student. Often the emotions involved in a confrontation let the teacher see frustration, inadequacy, anger, or fear. Hopefully this insight can be used to handle the student and salve his/her feelings.

Remember *what* you say is more important than *how loud* or *how long* it takes you to say it. Only say what you are willing to have quoted. Generally, be cautious when one person attempts to speak for others. This is an especially good ploy for the students who are attempting to play a game called, "Everybody Else." Deal only with what that individual says and get the facts before you take a stand involving others. Don't accept relayed quotes of other teachers, students, or administrators without verification. Be good at asking questions and getting at the *details* and *specifics,* not generalities. It is wise to write down what is said after the confrontation has subsided, and if it is serious, report the encounter to the principal. Later, if the issue resurfaces, you will have notes to refresh your memory. Attempt to put the conflict behind you and resolve to carry no grudge against the individual. Often teachers and students alike take affront to remarks by students as though they are meant as a personal attack. Be sure to carefully evaluate the issue before assuming it was meant to be taken personally.

Constructive confrontations can occur with parents and other teachers as well as administrators. The same dynamics apply in all situations. It is not unusual for the new teacher to be frightened and almost feel guilty when having the first parent conference over an issue. Teachers often feel they are being attacked, and sometimes this is true. Generally, in the public schools, this occurs in the principal's office, but sometimes the first contact is made by telephone. Above all, be prepared! If it involves a grade, bring the gradebook. If it involves a verbal confrontation, sit down and think through everything that happened. Refer to your notes on exactly what was said. If you have time before-hand, fill the principal in on the details of what happened. If you are being attacked, it is extremely important to have all parties present who were involved in the confrontation. Avoid being put in the position of defending yourself against "phantom" charges. Often, what the child has told the parent may have been somewhat distorted in an effort for the child to save face with the parents or to avoid possible punishment by the parents. Don't be caught in the middle if at all possible. So often the child is caught up in the self-fulfillment of the parent's dreams, and the disillusionment is often too much for the parents or child to accept. Remember, parents' egos are so involved with the accomplishment or lack of accomplishment of their children that they have difficulty being objective. Always maintain the posture of a helping attitude, and remember that the purpose of the conference is to help the child accomplish whatever the goal or task might have been. If you adopt a punitive attitude, your chances of support or respect from either the parent, child, or principal will diminish. If a problem occurs with a child, the parent should be brought into the picture as soon as possible. They are usually extremely helpful and provide much insight into the child.

Dealing with Discipline

Research seems to indicate discipline as the most common of all concerns of both new and experienced teachers alike.[7,8] The recommended reading list has many helpful suggestions for styles in disciplining students. Many different techniques can be used to your advantage, so let's concentrate on some guidelines which can help you to maintain discipline regardless of which chosen technique is implemented. Effective planning and teaching will eliminate most situations that evolve into discipline problems! The use of recognition and students' ideas can be of singular importance to your teaching. Make sure the praise fits the task and that this praise is given as soon after the desired behavior as possible. "Good" is no substitute for "That's an excellent serve, Judy!" Sometimes ignoring poor behavior, when it is not disruptive, gives you a chance to recognize a student's good performance later. We all need tender love and care. Give students the attention they need/deserve in acceptable ways or frequently they will demand it in unacceptable ways. An ounce of prevention is worth a pound of cure.

When you are attempting to change or shape the behavior of a student, watch the student to get a good profile of what is happening before you make your approach. Keep a written record and analysis of any reprimands used when dealing with the misbehavior of the child to let the student know you are watching and concerned about his/her actions. This is also helpful if you have to send the student from the classroom for discipline. The principal often takes the teacher more seriously when a written record appears to document the behavior. Be consistent in the types of infringements that are recorded. Too much documentation may equal harassment of the student and can be just as damaging as too little documentation. Make sure records are kept equally on all students, not just one. It is important to take the stance that the concern you have is to help the student be "better" and therefore attain higher achievement in class. By the way, this *really* should be why you are disciplining the child. To explain to the child that he/she is not allowed to run across the gym while going to team lines because you are concerned that he/she might be hurt is much better then because it is a rule. Don't feel that to give reasons is to communicate

---

[7]Charles, C. M. *Building Classroom Discipline*. New York: Longman, Inc. 1981.
[8]Long, J. D., and Williams, R. L. *SOS for Teachers*. Princeton, NJ: Princeton Book Company, 1982.

weakness on your part. It instead radiates a positive attitude of concern. The same applies when attempting to have the class emulate a desired behavior. "Mike and Sarah are ready for roll call!" is so much more positive than, "I'm not going to call roll until every one is quiet!" If a child is angry and abusive of other children, a time-out procedure might be helpful. Give the child a place to cool down and deal with him/her on a one-to-one basis while the class continues the activity.

Occasionally, a student will continue to present a problem to you and demand individual attention. As a teacher more and more time can be spent dealing with one student while 30 or 40 others are deprived of their classroom activity. *Do not let one student deprive you of time that will benefit the entire class.* Find ways to help the student be better outside of classtime. Be sure to recognize positive more than negative behavior in your class, and don't permit the negative behaviors to be more profitable than positive ones. If time-out procedures, extra positive attention, or one-on-one talks don't work, it may be time to involve the parents and administration. Attending to personal records of the misbehavior can ensure being on top of the problem.

Don't be afraid to take time to discipline before chaos develops. Far too many teachers attempt to talk when students aren't listening. If it is important for students to listen, it's also important for you to ensure listening by stopping the activity. You, as the teacher, must make the students aware that behaviors must be appropriate before activity can be resumed. Condescending preaching tactics never quite seem to accomplish the goal. Again the interrogative approach is essential. "Why is it important to listen to instructions?" "What could happen if . . .?"

The new teacher often hesitates to make students feel uncomfortable or risk losing their affection by being thought of as "mean" or unpleasant. Often misbehavior is ignored because of this feeling. Sometimes overwhelmed by the need to be accepted and liked by students, the teacher places himself/herself in a vulnerable position. However, respect is the emotion which should dominate the classroom. There will always be some students who may not like you. The teacher who is an affection-seeker gives the class the option to use rejection as a weapon. Watch out! Being interested in their well-being, showing a genuine interest in them, and being fair and consistent brings the new teacher much closer to being respected by the class. Affirming in your own mind what behavior is acceptable to you is imperative. Don't keep this a secret. As the unacceptable point is approached, let your students know. Don't wait for things to go "too far" and get out of hand.

Look closely at the informal leaders in the structure of the class. Are they working for you or against you? If your previous efforts to gain their respect have been futile, and you feel there is nothing more you can do to change this problem, remember, parents can be very helpful in working with you on their child's behavior. Don't overlook this assistance. The counselor or other teachers may also be able to give you additional insight into the problem. Don't give up, and continue to express an interest in the student.

Sometimes a teacher feels backed into a corner with overwhelming management problems with children. Above all, don't threaten unless you mean what you say. Invariably the teacher who depends on threats places himself/herself in a vulnerable position because the next one to misbehave may be the one who hasn't presented himself/herself as a problem all year. Using group disciplinary action for what mischief one or a handful have done is a quick way to encounter problems with your students. It is also a quick way to lose the respect of parents and administrators. No one likes to be disciplined for something one didn't do. Try to get all the facts and find out who is at the bottom of the problem before you discipline the class for the misbehavior. Stay calm. Until you have the facts don't take disciplinary action. The same idea applies when two people are involved in an incident. One initiated the conflict and the other is merely protecting himself/herself. Too many times the teacher is guilty of acting too hastily and disciplining both. This actually creates a problem rather than solving one. It reinforces the behavior of the aggressor.

Don't go out too far on your own and come up with unique ways of disciplining students. It's all right to be creative, but consult a good administrator before trying out anything that could be embarrassing or harmful to the student. The endorsement of the administration and possibly of the board members is absolutely necessary if intending to deviate from school policy. Also, make sure that the disciplinary action fits the offense. If you are attempting to instill values for physical fitness activities, using running as a disciplinary action is counterproductive to that goal. Additionally, if those students enjoy running, it is not unpleasant for them anyway.

Look for the good in students. This may sound like a difficult task. However, the most abusive, aggressive student who gives you the most trouble may also be the very one who makes an offensive or defensive strategy work that you have hoped the class would utilize in that activity. Compliment the student and reinforce appropriate behavior. Each individual brings unique and varying qualities, acceptable or unacceptable, to you and the class. You must take that extra step and look hard to find a quality that can be reinforced. Having been in that situation, recognizing something as simple as "I like that shirt you're wearing!" brought about the child wearing the same shirt two to three times a week. I continued with "There's that shirt I like again!" Whether the shirt had always been worn, or the student was increasing its wearing time to please me, the quality of interactions between student and teacher were quite different. Capitalize on your attention-seekers. Endorse the good thinking of the critic. At times learn to laugh with the clown. Serve all the students, not just the best and worst. Remember those who are in the comfortable, quiet middle.

If you are in a situation where you are away from the school grounds on a field trip or if the students are in a different part of the building, have a game plan drawn up for the students' behavior. Their behavior, whether good or bad, is a reflection on you, the teacher. Whether taking the students to the bowling alley or to participate in athletic competition, you are being judged by their actions. How nice it is to hear a restaurant manager who has just served your 25 students lunch say that this is the best behaved group of students he/she has seen. How terrible it is to have a call from the principal or superintendent who was informed by the motel where your team stayed that they will no longer allow the school to stay there. Invariably, the administrator will demand why you didn't have better control over the students? What about roller skating being dropped from the curriculum because the students were not taught to behave in the rink? Children are often expected to misbehave. *You, as the adult, are expected to have control over their behavior.* You will probably bear the consequences of any misbehavior. Have specific guidelines established *before* any trip occurs.

Handling the Paperwork

The overwhelming volume of paperwork can be distressing to the new teacher. Which form to use in which instance is almost as perplexing as how often one has to fill out a form. Roll-keeping is of utmost importance, particularly to schools that receive money for their pupils' attendance. That attendance is checked is important in itself, but accuracy is vitally imperative. The attendance sheet can also be used as a legal document in cases of truancy or court procedures. If equipment is to be ordered or repaired and facilities are to be maintained or upgraded, paperwork is generally required in the form of a purchase requisition or maintenance request. Keep copies of these for yourself to verify that action has been requested by you. Field trips or athletic contests away from the school grounds must have arrangements made on paper for purposes of cost accounting as well as to ensure the availability of a vehicle and driver. School records of test scores or special educational programs for special populations must be accurate and available for parents and other teachers alike. Official records of student skills tests, knowledge tests, daily grades, attendance, etc. must be accurately kept. Gradebooks and grade sheets are normally kept by the schools as documentation of student performance. Keeping up with the paperwork in terms of accuracy and being timely is vital. Teachers who keep thorough and accurate records of student performance and attendance are more apt to earn a good evaluation from the administrator. If that is one of your weak areas, take steps to correct it. Paperwork is demanding, but can be conquered. Take time to find out from your administrator, department chairperson, or athletic director which forms are necessary and how long in advance they must be submitted.

Recommended Readings

Kohut, S., and Range, D. G. *Classroom Discipline: Case Studies and Viewpoints*. Washington, DC: National Education Association, 1979.

Long, J. D., and Frye, V. H. *Making It till Friday*. 2d. ed. Princeton, NJ: Princeton Book Company, 1981.

Madsen, Jr., Charles H., and Madsen, Clifford K. *Teaching/Discipline: Behavioral Principles toward a Positive Approach*. Boston, MA: Allyn and Bacon, Inc., 1971.

3

Making a Difference: Functioning in the Organization

Can one teacher have an impact? Does what you do matter? Recent research has indicated that teachers who feel that their own efforts and behavior make a difference are more effective than those who feel that events are beyond their control. Teachers with a greater sense of efficacy or personal control produce higher levels of student achievement and are more likely to be innovative in their approaches to education.[1] They also tend to be satisfied with their career choice and remain in the teaching profession.

Making a difference will require some effort on your part. Not only will you need to continue to develop your teaching skills, you also will need to learn to effectively operate in the social system of the school. You have spent much of your life in schools, but now that you are a teacher your perspective will change. In some ways being on the other side of the desk will feel like being in a different world. As a new arrival, the first thing you will want to do is map out the terrain.

Understanding the System

A school is a mini-society with a life of its own. Like any community it has rules and norms, a power structure, social groups, rituals, and customs. Understanding the social system will help you fit in and possibly prevent errors on your part. Much of this you will learn informally, but it can be helpful to conduct a thoughtful, systematic examination.

In a social institution such as a school, members of the group have *roles* to play. A role is a position in the organization (principal, teacher, student, etc.) for which there is a set of norms defining how others expect the person to act.[2] You are changing from the role of student to that of teacher. Peoples' expectations of you have changed accordingly. If you return to the school from which you graduated, you might find that your "old" teachers still view you as a student. This may take a while to overcome. If you are a student-teacher, you may discover that one of the difficult things is knowing which role to play when.

---

[1]Sherman, T. M., and Giles, M. B. "The Development and Structure of Personal Control in Teachers." *Journal of Educational Research 74:* 139–42.

[2]Biddle, B. J. *Role Theory: Expectations, Identities and Behaviors.* New York: Academic Press, 1979.

Learning a new role is one of your major tasks as a new teacher. When we learn a new role we first must learn the norms or expectations which others have for the role—what is it that teachers do and don't do? Then our task is to personalize or adapt the role so that it fits our unique characteristics. Eventually the role becomes a part of us; we have integrated it into our belief system until it becomes a natural way for us to act.

Norms will define how persons in a particular role are expected to look and behave. Some norms are shared by all participants in the institution. For example, no member of the school is allowed to steal. Other norms are role-specific. Teachers may be able to strike students but students cannot strike teachers. Power may control what behavior is acceptable for one group as opposed to another, e.g., the principal may park illegally but teachers may not. Violations of a norm or expectation will usually result in some type of sanction or punishment from others in the group. Sanctions may be formal or informal and range from mild disapproval to severe punishment or even expulsion from the group.

Norms will vary somewhat from school to school. Teachers and students in one school may look and act very differently from those in another. To gain an understanding of the roles and norms in your school, list each of the key roles. Observe the behavior of people in those roles and the reactions of others to them. What are acceptable and unacceptable behaviors for each role? Are the expectations for physical education teachers the same as for other teachers in the school? In what ways do they differ?

Table 1. The role of the physical education teacher.

Based on your observations list the behaviors that are acceptable and unacceptable for physical education teachers in your school.

PE Teachers Do: **PE Teachers Don't Do:**

With which of the things listed do you feel most comfortable? Do any of them make you uncomfortable? Why?

What are the sanctions for not meeting these expectations?

In what ways do the expectations for physical education teachers differ from those for other teachers?

One of the things you may notice is that not everyone has the same set of expectations for a particular role. Administrators and students may have different expectations of teachers. Teachers may expect students to behave in one way and their peers may expect them to behave in another. Even different teachers have somewhat differing expectations of how students should behave. As a student teacher or new teacher, you may be caught in a struggle between those who believe students should be strictly regimented and those with whom "anything goes."

Such differing expectations or *intra-role conflicts* create a trade-off for the role occupant who cannot please everybody. Frequently the person will try to compromise or will respond to the people controlling the strongest sanctions. For the student who wants to go to college, this may mean choosing to meet the teachers' expectations, at least in class. For the student to whom grades are unimportant, acceptance or rejection by friends may be the more powerful influence. It is important to understand existing norms and expectations in dealing with students and with colleagues. You may be surprised at how different this school is from the one in which you were a student.

Another important aspect of understanding the system is to identify the power structure and affiliation networks which exist.[3] Power involves control over others and is reflected by control of access to valued resources and dispersal of rewards and punishment. Authority refers to power that is accepted by others as legitimate. A bully has power but not authority; an elected official or principal has both. When one's power is accepted by others as legitimate, it is rarely necessary to resort to force or threats of force.

Different roles in the school have differing amounts of power associated with them. In addition to administrators with official positions of authority, others have informal or unofficial power. The principal's secretary may have power because of controlling access to the principal. The janitor who controls heating and cooling systems, equipment, and room maintenance may wield considerable power over teachers. The high visibility of the football coach may give him more power than other teachers. The values of those in power often set the tone for the entire school. It is important to know who has power and what they value.

Identify which decisions are controlled by whom. Do others accept or question this authority? What means are used to enforce decisions? Is the power widely shared or narrowly held? How accessible are the persons with power?

One of the major tasks of new teachers is to be accepted by their students as having authority or legitimate power. The subject of power and authority makes many teachers uncomfortable. Much educational literature has denounced teacher authoritarianism and argued for increased student decision-making. However, it is clear that communities give teachers power and responsibility for the education of their children. Perhaps the resolution of this apparent dilemma requires focusing on authority, not power. If students accept the teacher as having authority (legitimate power), it is often because of the teacher's expertise and concern for students. Teachers who have gained such acceptance need not rely on threats and force to gain student compliance and can more readily share decision-making with students.

How does a new teacher gain student acceptance of his/her authority? In the past such acceptance may have been more or less automatically granted to all teachers, but currently each teacher must earn the respect of the students. It is a ritual in schools to test new teachers. To pass this test, the new teacher must exhibit three things: (1) expertise—knowing what you are talking about; (2) emotional control—avoiding both blowups and tears; and (3) concern for students—not a pal but a kind, fair, caring adult. It might be interesting to assess yourself each day on these three qualities. Passing marks are a good indication that you are gaining the authority of the teacher.

A concept closely related to power and authority is that of autonomy. While power refers to the ability to impose decisions on others, autonomy refers to the

---

[3]Schelechty, P. C. *Teaching and Social Behavior.* Boston, MA: Allyn and Bacon, 1976.

right to make decisions for oneself.[4] People have autonomy in one of two circumstances: those in power have officially granted them the right to make certain decisions; the lack of supervision permits them freedom of action. Even though teachers rarely have much power outside their classrooms, the isolation in which they work often provides them with considerable autonomy in their own classes. How much power and autonomy do you have in your school? Probably your autonomy is somewhat determined by your teaching situation. If you share facilities or team teach, you will have less autonomy than if you teach alone. The open facilities in which physical educators teach often make their work more visible than that of classroom teachers.

The affiliation network or friendship patterns among members of the school are also important. As in any social group, the bonds formed between friends will have an important influence on their behavior. In addition to affiliations with other teachers, some of your colleagues may have friendships or family ties with those in power such as the school board, school administrators, or city officials. You need to be aware of these personal loyalties because they can work for you or against you.

Initiating Change

As a new teacher, you may find many aspects of school routines and programs unfamiliar and uncomfortable. Things that other teachers take for granted may seem ineffective or undesirable to you. Your probable reaction will be to question the way things are done and to push for change. New ideas and perspectives are one of the important contributions of new teachers. However, efforts to create change require thoughtful deliberation and careful action if they are to succeed.

Examination of the source of your dissatisfaction is the first step. Why do I feel there is a need for change? Do I dislike this procedure because it is ineffective or because I feel insecure doing it? If I believe it is ineffective, do I have any evidence to back up my belief? Do others share my perception? Is it the system which needs changing or do I need to adjust to the system? Such self-examination is important because being an effective teacher requires being willing to change yourself as well as to change others.

In many cases you will probably conclude that changes in program or procedures are needed. Avoid the mistake of speaking up too quickly before you have had time to develop a plan of action. Because you hope to act as an agent for change, it is important to build your credibility in the school system. There are three factors influencing your credibility as a change agent: power; expertise; affiliations.[5]

A person with power and authority clearly has an advantage when attempting to implement change. However, a new teacher rarely has much power. The one realm in which you do have power and autonomy is your own classroom. Teachers have power over students and therefore can make

---

[4]Corwin, R. G., and Edelfeldt, R. A. "Life in Organizations." In *Perspectives on Organizations: Viewpoints for Teachers*, edited by T. E. Andrews and B. L. Bryant. Washington, DC: American Association of Colleges for Teacher Education, 1976, pp. 11–43.

[5]Huberman, A. M. *Understanding Change in Education: an Introduction*. Paris: UNESCO, 1973.

changes in the conduct of classes as long as such changes do not impact other teachers and school policy. However, it may be important to first gain student acceptance of your authority as a teacher before attempting any radical changes.

A second factor influencing your effectiveness in getting others to accept change is your perceived expertise. If others think you know what you are talking about, they are more likely to be influenced by you. Typically new teachers get somewhat mixed ratings in this area. Because of the recency of your education, you may be viewed as being current on certain topics. For example, you may be more knowledgeable about health-related fitness than older teachers. On the other hand new teachers are generally viewed as totally lacking in expertise in the "real world." Suggestions for change are likely to be met with skepticism and comments such as "That sounds fine but it won't really work."

Winning the respect of fellow teachers and administrators requires patience. You will need to prove yourself in the real world as well as demonstrate your mastery of subject matter content. Usually the critical test is your managerial ability. If others see that you can effectively organize and conduct classses and do not threaten or alienate them, they will be more willing to listen to your ideas.

The third aspect of your effectiveness as a change agent is the affiliatiohs or friendships you have with others in the system. People are more easily influenced by people they like. New teachers join a group in which affiliation patterns already exist. It takes time to win the friendship of your colleagues. Although you may have a natural tendency to make friends with other new teachers, be careful not to develop an "us and them" mentality.

In summary, patience is the key to building your credibility. Time and effort will allow you to gain student acceptance of your authority as a teacher and to win the respect and affection of your colleagues. Trying to change things too quickly will simply reduce the likelihood of success.

Once the time for initiating change has arrived, the key decision is selecting the right target. It is rarely wise to try to change everything at once! Timing is very important.

Two basic issues will underlie your choice of a target for change: How important is this problem?; Is it a manageable problem which can really be solved? Sometimes the most critical problems are the most resistive to change. In such cases it may be wise to select a less monumental problem which you think you can handle. If this is your first attempt at initiating change, you want to maximize your chances of success in order to build your confidence.

Your chances of success depend not only upon picking the right problem but also the right solution. Every problem has more than one possible solution. To avoid too narrow a view of the possibilities, list as many solutions as you can. Then evaluate each of your ideas by asking yourself three questions:

1. Is it practical in our situation? Do we have the staff, time, facilities, equipment, and money to implement the idea?
2. Will it get results? If we do implement it, will it solve the problem?
3. Is it acceptable to the people involved? Does it conflict with the norms and value systems of students, teachers, administrators, or parents? How might those in power positions feel about the proposed change? Would it fit in with your conception of their values?[6]

---

[6]Havelock, Ronald. *The Change Agent's Guide to Innovation in Education.* Englewood Cliffs, NJ: Educational Technology Publications, 1973.

No solution will be perfect on all three counts. You and your colleagues will have to make a judgment as to the solution which represents the best compromise.

Table 2. Evaluating alternative solutions.

Problem:
A large number of students are not dressing or participating in physical education class. According to current policy, after six such misses they fail the course.

Proposed Solutions:
1. Allow students more time for changing clothes at the beginning and end of class.
2. Allow students to participate in street clothes as long as they have tennis shoes.
3. Change the program so that students can choose activities of higher interest to them.
4. Initiate a reward system so that those with good participation get to participate in special activities (field trips, guest celebrity athletes, etc.).
5. Initiate a make-up assignment program so that students who have reached the failing mark can get a second chance.

List other possibilities:
6.
7.
8.

For each of the proposed solutions, evaluate the following:

    Practicality: Can we implement it?
    Benefit: Will it get results, that is, improve participation?
    Acceptability: Will teachers, students, and/or administrators accept it?

Which solution or solutions would you choose? Why?

Part of the process of initiating change is developing a strategy for when and how to approach others regarding your concern. One strategy is to get expansive and diverse involvement from the beginning so that everybody participates in the development of the proposed change. This is usually done by raising the problem at a meeting and asking what can be done about it. This participatory process has some advantages in that everyone involved probably will have a higher commitment to the eventual solution. However, this approach may not work in the absence of good leadership to help the group arrive at and implement a decision or in a situation with an autocratic administrator who is not responsive to group suggestions. An alternative is for you to develop a plan and then sell it to colleagues and administrators. The persuasion approach can be very effective if you do your homework and if you sell your idea to key people in the power structure first. One caution—remember that people make decisions on both rational and emotional bases. You need both convincing arguments and sensitivity to people's values, concerns, and insecurities.

The process of change in a complex social institution like a school is a slow step-by-step process. Adoption and diffusion of new ideas in any field of education including physical education takes a long time. Both patience and persistance are required if you are to make a difference.

Career Predators

Inherent in any organization are elements which are supportive and elements which are destructive of individual efforts. Awareness of these factors can help you succeed in countering their negative effect upon your career.

Stereotyping. One of the most destructive forces in any social system is stereotyping and prejudice. Stereotyping is the process of assuming that all members of a group have certain characteristics.[7] For example, common stereotypes include women are poor drivers, redheads have hot tempers, and athletes are dumb. Stereotypes are different than generalizations about the average member of a group. While the generalization that the average man is stronger than the average woman is true, it is a stereotype to assume that all men are strong and all women are weak. Individual differences exist within any group and the arbitrary assignment of the same traits to all members of the group is stereotyping. Teachers, like other people, often hold stereotypes of students, teachers, and administrators and treat them accordingly based on these preconceived notions about their abilities and behavior.

Table 3. Stereotyping.

I. List groups of which you are a member. For each group, list a stereotype about that group.

           Group   **Stereotype**

    Do you fit the stereotype listed for each of the groups? Do people treat you according to the stereotype or your individual characteristics? How do you react to stereotyping?

II. What are the stereotypes about each of these groups of students? Do you ever communicate these stereotypes by your actions?

           Group   **Stereotype**

    Girls
    Boys
    Blacks
    Hispanics
    Asians
    Athletes
    Handicapped
    Obese

Stereotyping can have many negative effects upon the individuals involved. One of the most damaging is that stereotyping can serve as the basis for prejudice or the tendency to "pre-judge" individuals because of traits they are assumed to have. Racial prejudice continues to be a pervasive problem in our society. Breaking the habit of stereotyping may be the key to avoiding prejudice and giving individuals a chance to prove themselves. Stereotyping may also lead to an intolerance for individuals who deviate from our stereotypic expectations. The girl who is an athlete and the boy who is a dancer may be rejected and ridiculed because they do not fit the accepted stereotypes. Efforts to reduce sexism are really attempts to eliminate stereotypes and to acknowledge and accept a range of individual differences among males and

---

[7]*Self Study Guide to Sexism in Schools*. Pennsylvania Department of Education, 1975.

females. The third way in which stereotyping can damage individuals has been called the self-fulfilling prophecy.[8] Because a stereotype can affect the individual's beliefs about self and other peoples' expectations for that person, the stereotype may have a tendency to come true. If we believe that girls can't handle math or that blacks can't learn to swim, our expectations may affect both their confidence and our ability to teach them.[9]

Your success and career satisfaction as a teacher require learning to avoid stereotyping. The first step in the process is increased self-awareness. Just as you want to be judged fairly on the basis of your individual merits, so do others!

Role Overload and Conflict. One of the factors which complicates our lives is that each of us occupies not just one but many social roles. You are not only a teacher but you may also be a spouse, a parent, a son or daughter, a community leader, etc. Because we occupy multiple roles simultaneously, we are subject to role overload and role conflict.[10] Sometimes a person simply does not have the time, energy, or ability to adequately fulfill all of the expectations associated with each of the roles held (role overload). In some cases fulfilling one role may directly contradict the expectations of another (role conflict).

Physical educators often experience role overload and role conflict within their jobs for most have not one but two occupational roles—teacher and coach.[11] Adequate performance in each of these roles requires considerable time and energy. Although the qualifications for the two may be similar, there are differences. Teachers deal with larger groups of less-skilled and perhaps less-motivated students in an instructional setting while coaches work with smaller groups of highly skilled, voluntary participants in a competitive setting. The demands of these two positions often produce a strain on the person trying to do both.

How does one deal with this conflict? Basically there are two different strategies. One is to decide that one of the roles is more important to you (the primary role) and that you are going to devote your time and energy to that role. If possible, the person making this decision withdraws from the other role. The physical educator who chooses teaching as a primary role may attain an elementary school position which does not require coaching. The one who chooses coaching may receive a full-time coaching position in a college. However, for many, such withdrawal is not possible because most secondary school and some elementary physical education jobs require both teaching and coaching. In this case, the withdrawal may be psychological. The person holds both positions but gives time and energy to the primary role and minimally performs the secondary role. This strategy will be successful only if it is consistent with the prevailing value system of the school. Because of the high value placed on athletics in our society, coaching most often becomes the primary role. Public recognition, pressure from parents, and emphasis by administrators all tend to reinforce this decision. Principals frequently attend

---

[8]Snyder, M. "Self-fulfilling Stereotypes." *Psychology Today* 16 (7): 60-8.

[9]Martinek, T. J. "Pygmalion in the Gym: a Model for Communication of Teacher Expectations in Physical Education." *Research Quarterly for Exercise and Sport* 52 (1): 58–67.

[10]Getzels, J. W., and Guba, E. C. "Role, Role Conflict, and Effectiveness." *American Sociological Review* 19: 164–75.

[11]Locke, L. F., and Massengale, J. D. "Role Conflict in Teacher/Coaches." *Research Quarterly* 49: 162–74.

athletic events and rarely visit the physical education program. Physical education classes are often ignored by the teacher and remarkably little sanction occurs from administrators, parents, or students for this action. However, choosing this strategy may have long-term negative effects on your career. Because of the time requirements, emotional demands, and emphasis upon winning in competitive athletics, few people continue coaching throughout their careers. The coach who has ignored teaching may find life without coaching empty and unsatisfying.

The alternative strategy for dealing with role overload and conflict is to reach a compromise which attempts to fulfill the expectations of both roles. This strategy requires a perspective which permits reasonable limits to be set for each: I will do the best I can as a teacher and a coach—up to a point. To the fullest extent possible, the two roles are integrated. I try to learn things I can use in both. At the same time, boundaries are drawn. This is my teaching time and I don't use it to plan practices or work with athletes. Time shortcuts become important to survival. Perhaps the key to the success of this strategy is receiving rewards and satisfactions from both roles. The rewards associated with athletics are very potent and visible. You may need to seek ways to feel rewarded for your teaching. Recognize that if you care about both teaching and coaching, you will want to feel that others do too. Find a support system to help you. Appreciative students, other teachers in the school, or professional colleagues outside the school can provide positive reinforcement for your efforts.

Bureaucracy. A bureaucracy is an organization which is characterized by hierarchical authority and inflexible routines, rules, and regulations. As school systems get larger and more complex, they tend to become more bureaucratic.[12] Teachers are often overwhelmed by endless recordkeeping and paperwork and by policies and procedures dealing with seemingly trivial aspects of daily life. The frustrations of working in a bureaucracy include the time required for reporting and communication, the impersonal qualities of standardized procedures, and the resistance of the organization to change. Bureaucratic administrators are reluctant to make exceptions for individual cases and often justify decisions on the basis of precedent or "going by the book." Individuals are expected to conform and are viewed as somewhat interchangeable parts of the system.

How does one survive in such an atmosphere? How do you maintain your feelings that your actions and judgment as a professional make a difference? In part, you do this by learning to impact the system, to act as a change agent as was previously discussed. The other part of surviving in a bureaucracy is developing your zone of autonomy, that area of your work in which you have independence and control. One of the major factors influencing teacher's autonomy is the amount of supervision which exists. During their probationary period, beginning teachers are likely to be monitored closely for both competence and conformity. Once the administration has judged the teacher as eligible for ongoing employment, the amount of supervision will be reduced giving the teacher increasing latitude and personal autonomy. Teachers frequently learn that their zone of autonomy may allow them to control meaningful educational decisions as long as they conform in less significant

---

[12]Corwin and Edelfeldt, 1976.

routines. One experienced teacher says that "If my attendance records are accurate and I avoid serious discipline problems, they let me teach the way I want to . I just stay out of their way and do my own thing." Although some view the absence of supervision of teachers as a problem, the authors' view is that autonomy and responsible decision-making are inherent to a satisfying professional career.

Most teachers define success in terms of the impact they have on students' behavior.[13] Knowing that you can make a difference is essential to a satisfying and successful career in education. Making a difference requires both personal teaching skills and the opportunity to use those skills effectively. Understanding the social system of the school may enable you to establish a situation which provides such an opportunity.

Recommended Readings

Corwin, R. G., and Edelfeldt, R. A. "Life in Organizations." In *Perspectives on Organizations: Viewpoints for Teachers,* edited by T. E. Andrews and B. L. Bryant. Washington, DC: American Association of Colleges for Teacher Education, 1976, pp. 11–43.

Doyle, W., and Ponder, G. "The Ethic of Practicality: Implications for Curriculum Development. In *Curriculum Theory,* edited by A. Molnar and J. A Zahork. Washington, DC: Association for Supervision and Curriculum Development, 1977.

Massengale, J. D. "Occupational Role Conflict and the Teacher/Coach." *Physical Educator 34,* 64–9.

Palmatier, Larry L. "How Teachers Can Innovate and Still Keep Their Jobs." *Journal of Teacher Education 26:* 60–2.

Snyder, M. "Self-fulfilling Stereotypes." *Psychology Today 16*(7): 60–8.

---

[13]Harootunian, B., and Yarger, G. P. *Teachers' Conceptions of Their Own Success.* Washington, DC: ERIC Clearinghouse on Teacher Education, 1981.

4

Learning to Cope: Staying on the Job

Because teachers constantly deal with a large number of individuals, they experience more potential stressors than the average layperson on a job. It is important for the teacher to face stress and *do something about it*. Not only must you be knowledgeable about sources of stress, but you must also be aware of the reactions to stress as a foundation for the possible options that your adjustments might take. It is also important for you to realize that the students' behaviors may be stress-based. Therefore, understanding the dynamics of stress and coping may help you to adjust as well as aid you in your ability to respond to students.

As you prepare to teach, you will be confronted with various tasks which require immediate attention. Not only is the new teacher adjusting to a new environment, new working conditions, new constraints on time, and possibly new living conditions, but the new teacher is expected to handle job-related problems without interference from outside forces. Concerns begin to build while an enormous number of tasks present themselves in the teaching profession. Some of the instructional duties which may be faced include large numbers of students, lack of supplies, teaching unfamiliar content, routines and schedules, and extracurricular coaching activities. It is expected that you will learn how to cope with these tasks in an effective and efficient manner. The new teacher, feeling inadequate already, begins to function in a constantly changing and demanding environment.

As you settle into the teaching profession, you begin to undergo subtle changes which actually are transforming you into the type of person you believe the situation demands. This is just one part of the socialization process that is taking place as one adapts to a new job. You are making personal adjustments which are necessary for you to fit comfortably within the structure of the job. This adjustment to the situation (the school and job) usually follows one of two options: compliance; internalization.[1]

In compliance you are merely accepting what the chairperson or the one in power, i.e., principal, athletic director, defines the job to be with all its constraints. Privately, however, you have reservations about the situation, and

---

[1]Lacy, C. *The Socialization of Teachers*. London: Methuen and Co., Ltd., 1977.

37

you view your task as "fitting in" or not "making waves." A compliance response can turn those natural high feelings of enthusiasm and excitement about the job to defiance or despondency if you aren't careful. Your ability to carry off the charade may determine your success with this position. You are truly playing a role and you cannot be transparent to those in power.

Compliance is a difficult position to maintain, but showing your discontent could have disastrous effects. It may be necessary for student teachers to comply if they wish to have good rapport with the school-based teacher, to successfully complete the internship, and to receive good recommendations for certification. Any hint to the supervising teacher that the student teacher is fault-finding may damage the sharing process. The new teacher may face the same dilemma. The power person (administrator, principal, athletic director) must not detect discontent if the new teacher wants to remain at that school on contract. For a short period of time, compliance may not be too difficult. However, if your feelings are strong and far from compromising, additional adjustments will need to be made.

The other form of adjustment to a new role is internalization. In internalized adjustment the individual not only complies with the constraints of the job but believes they are for the best. He/she is really "fitting in" and "good," not merely pretending. Obviously, this is the best position, and this is probably what every new teacher desires. However, this doesn't mean the new teacher has it made, and no problems exist. It is simply much easier on a personal level to continue in a situation in which you believe.

Regardless of the form of initial adjustment, eventually a crisis occurs which may cause one to fail to get by. Being in risk or crisis situations calls for self-appraisal and self-examination, but the direction it takes is not necessarily automatic.[2] The individual can, however, make use of a crisis to improve future performance. Most people can take a fair amount of criticism without disturbing their self-esteem or creating self-delusion. However, the new teacher is often more vulnerable because he/she has strong feelings of inadequacy.[3] A crisis also calls for efforts to preserve one's self-image and often forces the individual into a "security mentality" or defensive posture which helps to protect the new teacher from discomfort. Dynamically, the individual is attempting to regain personal equilibrium and does so by finding alternate solutions to the problem that preserve his/her self-image. If self-image is not preserved, the individual then becomes frustrated and tension increases.[4] If the new teacher's customary response to a problem fails, he/she generally depends on alternate adjustments to accomplish the task.

When confronted with various situations or problems of stress in teaching, the teacher must react in some fashion. The individual usually reacts either by some form of attack, withdrawal, or compromise. Attack responses commonly involve direct action, and the kind of action often depends on whether pressure, frustration, or conflict is a part of the stress.[5] Withdrawal reactions may be very

---

[2]Lindesmith, A. R., and Strauss, A. L. *Social Psychology*. 3d ed. Dallas, TX: Holt, Rinehart, Winston, 1968.

[3]Wendt, J. C.; Bain, L. L.; and Jackson, A. S. "Fuller's Concerns Theory as Tested on Prospective Physical Educators." *Journal of Teaching Physical Education,* Spring, 1981, pp. 66–70.

[4]Shibutani, T. *Society and Personality*. Englewood Cliffs, NJ: Prentice-Hall, Inc., 1961.

[5]Coleman, J. C., and Hammen, C. L. *Contemporary Psychology and Effective Behavior*. Glenview, IL: Scott, Foresman and Co., 1974.

appropriate if the situation exerts demands that cannot or should not be met. Compromising reactions to stress use substitution and accomodation to adjust to the problem. Most task-oriented behavior is compromising because of the satisfaction involved in the maneuver.

Such adjustments, whether conscious or unconscious, are ways to cope with tension and stress and to preserve self-esteem. Both constructive and destructive coping mechanisms exist, and often the success of a career depends on the teacher's choice of such mechanisms. Some adjustments can be very destructive or dysfunctional to the individual and cause additional problems whereas others can help allieviate additional tension or stress. New teachers must be able to recognize dysfunctional coping mechanisms which are generally counterproductive and defensive in nature.

Patterns which alleviate the crisis in a constructive manner are generally sanctioned patterns of behavior which do not usually place the individual in a vulnerable position. For example, when having an ideological disagreement with a student, tactfully making your point and acknowledging the student's position, shows mutual respect and may keep the disagreement from turning into an argument. Some conventionally sanctioned tactics for preserving self-image are consciously utilized. Physical withdrawal (walking away), swapping favors, changing the subject, flattering, creating diversions, stalling for time, and exploiting the vulnerable points of the attacker are a few of the common ploys used to assuage a potential crisis.[6] Used in moderation these can be successful ways to cope with various situations. Detachment is one of the most effective ways of maintaining self-esteem. By maintaining a front consisting of a sense of humor, the ability to look at one's shortcomings, weaknesses, and mistakes, and joke or take the issue lightly makes one's involvement seem less serious.

When constructively coping with problems, the old military adage, "scout out the terrain and survey the situation" is a good guideline. If you impulsively handle a crisis without getting all the facts, you may regret it later. Review the Chapter 2 section on handling a confrontation for constructive patterns of problem-solving. It is very important to be a good listener and to know what's going on. Being in class as the students arrive cuts down on the myriad of problems that can develop if you are not present. Put your energy and effort into appropriate issues, and don't get caught up in shallow side skirmishes that may have little to do with the smooth operation of the class. Take the offensive to prevent or solve problems, and maintain objectivity without being defensive. Avoid taking personal affront to each issue that develops. If necessary share the problem with those who can give you advice and help. Design your class to be interesting and challenging. Adopt a teaching style compatible with your personality. If you can, be approachable. Change the routine occasionally, and maintain an interest in the ideas of your students, giving them input as often as is practical. Using constructive patterns of coping will help you experience the satisfaction of a career in teaching and gain the support of the students, parents, and administration.

Destructive or dysfunctional patterns also tend to alleviate a crisis but places the user in a vulnerable position—possibly physically and psychologically. These patterns can create the greatest problem for the new teacher. They merely make one feel better temporarily, but the primary problem

---

[6]Lindesmith and Strauss, 1968.

39

is still unresolved. Selective inattention or "tuning out," evasion of responsibility, rationalization, pretense, disowning of undesirable qualities in oneself, and anxiety reduction are all mechanisms of self-defense used to preserve self-image.[7] Whether they are always dysfunctional depends on their usage and the severity of the problem. However, the teacher often is not aware that the coping device is being used.

Other examples of various destructive adjustment patterns may be helpful. The use of misplaced aggressions may be a potential problem. The teacher may be a constant critic of the administration, faculty, and students or become an authoritarian disciplinarian and take out his/her aggressions on the students. Another potentially destructive way to deal with a problem may be for the teacher to collectivize or share the problem with a group of individuals who attempt to legitimize the displacement of blame. This approach is similar to students who perform poorly on a test rallying together and making their collectively poor showing the result of a bad test or a poor teacher. One device may find the teacher attempting to keep the problem quiet or possibly even refusing to admit that a problem exists. Rather than to appear incompetent or not on top of "things," the teacher attempts to avoid the problem causing a potentially destructive situation without producing a solution. Withdrawing from a situation can be a problem if overwhelming issues lead to a feeling of failure. This can also lead to on-the-job retirement or the paycheck syndrome in which the faculty member is interested only in picking up the monthly paycheck. Selling out on professionalism by "babysitting" one's classes or having shallow class activities to pass the time of day are often the first steps toward withdrawal. What about the feeling that the administrator is looking over your shoulder? In moderation this is probably healthy; however if it is extreme, it may border on paranoia. Extreme rigidity and/or territoriality such as "my gym" or "my class" can be counterproductive to effective coping. A compulsive organizer may have the same problem, and on an unconscious level the individual is often unaware that it is a coping device. Each of these responses to stress is destructive and places the new teacher in a vulnerable position. Table 1 provides a sample problem-solving response to a stress-related problem. Table 2 provides a worksheet on which you can analyze possible responses to your own task-oriented stressful situation. Even though reactions and decisions are often made quickly or on an unconscious level, taking time to look at a potential problem and analyzing your possible reactions may help you to handle them more constructively when they occur.

The basic steps necessary for coping with stress or any problem are: (1) to define and accept the problem as a challenge; (2) to work out alternative solutions and decide on a course of action; (3) to take action and avoid decision by indecision; and (4) to evaluate the feedback.[8] Decision by indecision often occurs when one fails to act in time to solve a problem. The task-oriented approaches of attack, withdrawal, and/or compromise are usually the most practical ways to work through stress and usually have the best chances of conflict resolution. However, factors beyond the control of the individual and faulty values may be stumbling blocks to success.[9]

---

[7]Ibid., 1968.
[8]Coleman and Hammen, 1974.
[9]Ibid., 1974.

Table 1. Worksheet for task-oriented reactions to stress.

Problem: Options for handling the accusation of poor classroom management.
Listed below are some of the possibilities in reacting to the above problem. See if you can think of any other possible reactions. Remember categories are not always discreet.

	Constructive	Destructive
ATTACK	Ask for specifics. Examine evidence. Determine cause. Take corrective action. Consult others. Maintain objectivity.	Blame students. Blame parents. Be punitive. Seek scapegoats.
WITHDRAW	Admit to problem. Back off and study.	Refuse help. Quit job. Control the way in which the problem is perceived.
COMPROMISE	Get help. Re-evaluate situation.	Value control—not teaching.

Table 2. Worksheet for task-oriented reactions to stress.

Problem: _____

	Constructive	Destructive
ATTACK		
WITHDRAW		
COMPROMISE		

All of this sounds so logical and rational, but stress is often camouflaged and has a way of sneaking up on the new teacher. Stress is often irrational and habit-oriented. Even in knowing the dynamics of problem-solving, there is no guarantee that new teachers will be able to use this knowledge personally and be aware of pending stress. It is also difficult to differentiate between stress and emotional dependency on other people. No two teachers have identical stress tolerances or identical reactions to stress.

Being knowledgeable about the sources and reactions to stress includes being in touch with your own feelings. Self-awareness is important for coping with stress as well as enabling personal growth. (See Chapter 5 for self-awareness and personal growth.) How you feel about yourself and teaching is very important. Through experience, values and goals become a part of our self-identity. Social change as it affects social norms and roles may actually cause us to restructure our self-concept to include characteristic ways of experiencing and feeling, i.e., being anxious, concerned, alienated, etc.[10] Individuals may actually internalize inadequacy as part of self. Psychologists believe that self-awareness is inherently curative and only awareness can lead to growth, change, and full-functioning.[11] "Change occurs when one becomes what he/she is, not when one tries to become what he/she is not."[12] Self-awareness then is extremely important if teachers are to function to their fullest potential within the framework of the school setting.

How do you feel about your abilities? What are your strengths? What are your limitations? What can you do to transfer these limitations to the strength column of your ledger? How do you feel about: approval by your students, peers, administrators; your abilities as a teacher; your general security; affection from your students; affection from a student for whom you don't particularly care; abusive students; your multi-cultural students; handicapped individuals; athletes; following directions; working with those with whom you are philosophically different; etc.? Many of these answers aren't fully handled on a conscious level by the new teacher. However, it would be wise to think these through and decide how you might react if faced with each issue. This might help you avoid being caught in an unpleasant situation.

To cope in the public school setting and to make the transition a little easier, teachers should have the ability to analyze problems. You need to be able to detect problems as well as admit that they exist. How accurately do you perceive the problem? How much of your perception of the situation is need-directed thinking? Where does optimism, pessimism, and realism fit into the solution?

Teachers should also develop outside interests as a diversion and a hedge against "burn-out." Escapism is not the answer because sometimes one is consumed by outside interests and evades problems. Yet, you can become institutionalized if no outside interests exist. Sometimes during stress it is best not to associate with colleagues during leisure time. Personal problems and professional problems should be kept separate. A bad teaching situation can affect one's personal life or vice-versa. Extra time should be spent in planning and organizing on Sunday evenings to ensure that the upcoming week's activities will go as smoothly as possible.

Various adjustments need to be made. "Now" persons must learn to cope with delays because schools may not be among society's fastest changing institutions. Because one unconsciously gravitates to companions and activities that permit weaknesses to remain hidden, it is important to have professional friends who will be critics and consultants to tell you the truth when wrong or

[10]Ibid., 1974.

[11]Ibid., 1974.

[12]Beisser, A. "The Paradoxical Theory of Change." In *Gestalt Therapy Now,* edited by J. Fagan and P. L. Shepart. Palo Alto, CA: Science and Behavior Books, Inc. 1977, pp. 77–80.

when behavior is stress-oriented. It is also important to spend time with those who encourage you by complimenting you when things go well and/or progress is being made. By developing a network of professional relationships where a healthy interchange of ideas can occur, the new teacher can develop alternatives for action.

New situations are challenging. Pace yourself. Many times the wind will be to your back while at other times you may head right into it. Your strength to handle these various situations should increase as you tune in and increase your own awarensss. When we perceive we can then plan for effective action. Finish your race strong.

Recommended Readings

Bellanca, J. A. *Values and the Search for Self*. Washington, DC: National Education Association, 1975.

Sparks, D., and Hammond, J. *Managing Teacher Stress and Burnout*. Washington, DC: ERIC Clearinghouse #SPO17376, 1981.

Wendt, J. C. "Coping Skills, a Goal of Future Preparation." *Proceedings: 1982 NAPEHE Annual Convention*. San Diego, CA. 1982, pp. 98–100.

Wlodkowski, R. J. *Motivation and Teaching: a Practical Guide*. Washington, DC: National Education Association, 1978.

5

Staying Alive: Personal Growth

Since we were children most of us have envisioned adulthood as having arrived at our destination. Our period of growth is behind us; we are now "grown-up." Recently we have begun to realize that personal growth and development continues throughout adulthood. Popular books like *Passages*[1] have described predictable crises and changes of adult life. As a beginning teacher you are probably a young adult. The next few years will be the ones of transition as you establish a career and a home. Most teachers are familiar with the process of child development. Understanding the development of adults may help you to enhance your own personal growth.

Developmental theorists have proposed that individuals have basic styles or problem-solving strategies which determine the way they interact with the environment and that these styles change at different stages of development. Each of us goes through similar stages but we move at our own rate and may stabilize or stop our development before realizing the higher stages. Higher stages are characterized by more abstract thinking, greater creativity and flexibility, increased ability to deal with complexity and stress, and greater empathy.[2]

Several people have examined the development of teachers. Fuller and her colleagues identified three stages of teacher development.[3] The first is the survival stage during which the teacher's concerns are self-directed: surviving; managing; getting through the day. The second stage has been called the mastery stage. The teacher's preoccupation is with acquiring teaching skills and mastering subject-matter content. The third stage is the stage of impact where the teacher begins to be concerned about what the students need and whether the instruction is having a positive impact on students.

While Fuller's work has focused on teachers' professional development, others have examined teachers' personal development and its relationship to

[1]Sheehy, G. *Passages*. New York: E. P. Dutton, 1974.

[2]Glassberg, S. "A Developmental Model for the Beginning Teacher." In Howey, K. R., and Bents, R. H., *Toward Meeting the Needs of the Beginning Teacher*. Minneapolis, MN: Midwest Teacher Corps Network, 1979.

[3]Fuller, F., and Bown, O. "Becoming a Teacher." In *Teacher Education*, seventy-fourth yearbook of The National Society for the Study of Education, edited by K. Ryan. Chicago, IL. University of Chicago Press, 1975.

their teaching performance. In general, these studies have shown that teachers at higher developmental levels tend to be flexible, tolerant, and are able to use a wide range of teaching styles.[4]

It seems clear that professional and personal growth will enhance your career as a teacher. You will want to learn new instructional strategies and managerial skills and to strengthen your expertise in your field. You will also want to attain emotional maturity and an open-mindedness which enables you to deal with complex issues and problems.

Strategies for Promoting Personal Growth

Self-awareness is fundamental to the process of personal growth. Such awareness requires being in touch with your present experience—what you feel, need, think, imagine, and sense. Many of the strategies for promoting personal growth involve activities designed to increase awareness of your experiences, your personal concerns, and the environmental factors which have influenced your personal development. Several examples of such activities are included in this chapter and in the recommended readings. You are encouraged not to merely read the descriptions but to do the activities. Personal growth is an active process requiring your involvement.

One aspect of getting to know yourself better is awareness of what you value, of what you think is important. An approach to doing this is to keep a values journal as described in Table 1. Such a journal recording your thoughts and feelings can provide both catharsis and insight. Keeping a journal requires a long-term commitment to personal growth. Other self-awareness activities may also be able to be done in a shorter time span. An example described in Table 2 examines feelings and preferences related to physical activity. This exercise may give you insight into the way you approach physical education.

Another important aspect of personal development is recognition and acceptance of feelings as a legitimate part of the total self. The activity in Table 3 is intended to help you bring your feelings to a conscious level by verbalizing them to yourself. You are also encouraged to explore the relationship between your thoughts and feelings and your behavior.

The exercise in Table 4 will help you examine the extent to which you disclose your feelings and thoughts to others. Sharing with others can increase your level of awareness and can provide you with emotional support. This support seems essential to the process of personal growth.

Based upon these self-awareness activities, you are encouraged to develop a plan for personal growth. The activity described in Table 5 is intended to help you develop such a plan. You are encouraged not only to determine your goals for personal growth but to identify the resources available to assist you in attaining them.

Strategies for Promoting Professional Growth

Professional growth is not automatic. It requires that the individual exist in an environment which is stimulating and challenging. As a teacher, how do you

---

[4]Glassberg, 1979.

Table 1. Values Journal.*

The format for a *Values Journal* is direct and quick. Write down some thoughts of importance to you at various intervals, perhaps once a day or twice a week. *Values Journal* entries are usually made for three months or more. Looking back, these entries will indicate something of the pattern and texture of your life and of your thinking over that period.

Contact a friend, selecting someone whose value-thoughts you are eager to hear. After two or perhaps three weeks, review and discuss with your friend all value-thoughts as they are clarified by these questions. Which of the *Values Journal* entries reflect your most cherished beliefs or attitudes? Which entries would you want to rewrite drastically at this moment?

In view of the *Values Journal* listings, try to make some summary statements about the following aspects of yourself and your life.

1. How do I, taking an average day as a spin-off, generally spend my time?

2. What are the things (at least five) that really interest me?

3. How do I view life as a whole? Is my outlook conditioned by influences outside myself?

4. What short-range and long-range goals can I honestly identify? What, ultimately, do I want to accomplish?

5. What are my primary commitments in life? (List in order of importance.)

6. What are some options that I reflect on, mull over, or enjoy imagining about?

7. Specifically, what five things do I most value about my life?

8. What conflicts or problems do I have about my life? Which ones did I personally create for myself and which ones are primarily caused by persons and situations outside my responsibility and control?

---

*Simon, S. B. *Meeting Yourself Halfway*. Niles, IL: Argus Communications, 1974. For information about current Values Realizations materials and a schedule of nationwide training workshops, contact Sidney B. Simon, Old Mountain Road, Hadley, MA 01035.

Table 2. Activities I enjoy.

List on the chart below ten sport or dance activities you enjoy doing. Put an * by your three favorite activities.

Activity	People	Competition	Vigor	Skill	Frequency	Age	Future
1.							
2.							
3.							
4.							
5.							
6.							
7.							
8.							
9.							
10.							

For each activity listed, indicate in the appropriate column the following information which describes the circumstances under which you do the activity and how you feel about it.

People: Alone, two, or group.

Competition: Formal (league, tournament, etc.), informal, none.

Vigor: High, medium, low (estimate physical demand based on the way you play).

Skill: Proud, OK, needs improvement (indicate how you feel about your present skill).

Frequency: Indicate how often you participate in the activity.

Age: Indicate your age when you began doing this activity.

Future: Indicate age when you expect to stop participating in this activity.

Table 3. Here and Now Wheels.*

Step 1. Describing thoughts, feelings, and behaviors.

Here and Now Wheel. In this activity, you are asked to complete a minimum of three "Here and Now Wheels." The purpose of this activity is to help you become aware of your own thoughts, feelings, and physical sensations as you are experiencing them. Each Here and Now Wheel represents your reactions to a different experience. In each you will find three circles which have been divided into quarters. Either before and/or after significant personal or classroom encounters, complete one Here and Now Wheel.

1. Circle A. *Here and Now Thoughts.*
   In each of the quadrants write one sentence that describes exactly your *thoughts* in anticipation of, or as a result of, a personal experience. What are the sentences that are going through your mind? For example, if you know that at three o'clock you have to face an irate mother who is coming to speak with you about her daughter's work, you may be thinking:

   I.   "Oh, no, not her again."
   II.   "I have to be at the doctor's by 3:30."
   III. "I have to think of something nice to say."
   IV.   "I'm glad she is showing some concern for her daughter."

2. Circle B. *Here and Now Feelings.*
   In each quadrant of the second circle place one word that describes your present *feelings.* For example, the teacher awaiting the angry parent's visit might enter the following feelings:

   I.   "Put upon."
   II.   Anxious.
   III. Annoyed.
   IV.   Pleased.

   The next step is to expand one of those words into several sentences. For example, the phrase "put upon" could be expanded into these sentences: "I feel put upon when she comes to visit me so often. I wonder if she doubts my competence as a teacher."

3. Circle C. *Here and Now Physical Sensations and Behaviors.*
   In each of the quadrants place a word that describes present *physical sensations and/or behaviors* that result from a particular experience. Again, the stimulus of the angry parent's visit might cause the teacher to feel or act:

   I.   Fidgety (playing with hair).
   II.   Sweaty.
   III. Stomach "talking."
   IV.   Relaxed.

---

*Cooper, J. M., et. al. *Classroom Teaching Skills: a Workbook.* Lexington, MA: D.C. Heath and Company, 1977.

Then expand one of the physical sensations or actions into a sentence. An example could be: "I feel so fidgety that I can't sit still."

Now ask yourself:

1. How easy or difficult was it for you to inventory and describe your thoughts, feelings, and physical sensations?
2. Which was the easiest to describe? Which was the most difficult?
3. What did you learn about yourself as a result of the experiences?
4. How could you adapt such an experience for use in your classroom?

To continue your own inventory process, answer the following questions.

Step 2. Identifying patterns.
1. What stimuli usually trigger such thoughts, feelings, and actions?
2. How do you usually act in such situations? What do you do? Say? What is your body "saying"?
3. In what other situations did you act in similar ways?

Step 3. Identifying consequences.
1. What are the consequences of responding that way?
2. How does it serve you to act that way?
3. What does it protect you from?
4. What does it help you to avoid?

If you choose, try to think of alternative modes of behavior—ones that may be more congruent with your goals. For example, in dealing with the previously described irate mother, if you usually become anxious and you consider that to be unproductive behavior, "try on" a new one—count to ten, smile, and then begin the conversation.

"Here and Now Wheels"

A. *Here and Now Thoughts.*

Circle A

I. _____
II. _____
III. _____
IV. _____

B. *Here and Now Feelings.*

Circle B

I. _____
II. _____
III. _____
IV. _____

Expanded Sentence

_____
_____
_____
_____

C. *Here and Now Physical Sensations.*

Circle C

I. _____
II. _____
III. _____
IV. _____

Expanded Sentence

_____
_____
_____
_____

Table 4. Disclosing thoughts and feelings to others.*

The purpose of this activity is to help you become more aware of your personal pattern of disclosure. Specifically, it will help you identify those persons *with whom* you may choose to share information about yourself as well as describe *what* type of information you would be willing to disclose to those selected persons.

In the figure below four concentric circles have been labeled with the words *Self, Intimates, Friends,* and *Acquaintances.* Try to conceptualize this diagram as an image of yourself and persons with whom you interact. If you place yourself in the center of all that happens around you, then those persons whom you allow to get the closest to you, in both physical and psychological proximity, would be called *intimates.* Those persons who are not as close as intimates, but are still at "arm's length," would be called *friends.* Those persons in the outer layer of your "world" would be *acquaintances.*

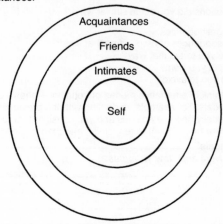

Privacy Blocks

1. Now, list the names of two or three persons that would fall in each of those categories. Ask yourself, "*To whom* would I be willing to disclose information about myself?" Then place their initials in the appropriate square.
2. Then ask yourself, "*What* information would I be willing to disclose?" Make a note on the type of information you would probably be willing to share with them. This information could reflect *feelings* (you feel lonely), *actions* (whom you voted for in the last election), or *thoughts* (your opinions of your job or your boss).
3. Now look at the categories of information listed below. Ask yourself, "At what relationship level would a person have to be in order for me to share this type of information?" Write each letter in the outermost appropriate circle. For example, if you were willing to tell almost anyone about your religious beliefs, place the letter *m* in the "acquaintance" circle. If you weren't willing to share your daydreaming with anyone, place the letter *a* in the "self" circle. Look at each category carefully, and allow yourself to honestly assess how comfortable you would feel sharing this information with others.
    a. Your daydreams.
    b. Your fantasies for the future.
    c. Your relationship with your parents.
    d. Your need to be a leader.
    e. Qualities that you don't like about yourself.
    f. Your fears of not being liked by other persons.
    g. Your fears of failure.
    h. Things of which you are proud.

*Cooper, J. M., et. al. *Classroom Teaching Skills: a Workbook.* Lexington, MA: D.C. Heath and Company, 1977.

i. Things that make you happy.
j. Your feelings of loneliness.
k. Your feelings of inadequacy.
l. Your marital relationship.
m. Your religious beliefs.
n. Your feelings about death.

4. Take a few moments to look over your categorization. Make changes if necessary.
5. Put an asterisk (*) in the circle that describes your relationship with the majority of your students.
6. Now look at the categories of information that you would disclose to people at that level. Would you be willing to share those categories of information with your students? Obviously, the age and level of sophistication of your students may limit the type of information you may choose to disclose, but ask yourself the following questions: "Do I ask my students to share this type of information with me?" "Am I treading into their area of privacy?" "Would I feel comfortable sharing the same information about myself?" "Is there reciprocal disclosure in my classroom?"
7. How private a person are you? Are there many categories of information that you placed in the "self" circle? In the "acquaintance" circle?
8. Where on the following continuum is your overall level of comfort in disclosing information about yourself with your students best described?

**Very
Uncomfortable**   **Very
Comfortable**

9. Share your responses with a friend. Are you comfortable with your present level of disclosure? What is your general pattern of behavior? How does it serve you to be this way? What does it get you? What does it help you avoid? When was the last time that disclosing information was productive? Unproductive?

Table 5. I Resolve.*

I Resolve . . . depends on much that has gone before. Refer to your *Values Journal* notations. What do your *discoveries* tell you about yourself?

What resolutions are you willing to make, able to make?

Everyone wants his or her resolutions to stick; everyone starts with such good intentions, but so often there's a slip 'twixt the promise and the practice.

Here's a method of ranking resolutions that will help you grade them on a personal-gain basis. Take a piece of paper and divide it into three vertical columns. In the first column list all the resolutions you have made, or need to make—*all* of them— or as many as you can think of, past, present, and future. Your resolutions may include a change in behavior, something you wish to learn, a new skill you might want to acquire, or new ways of getting along better with other people, etc.

In the second column, briefly list what you think you will gain if the resolution in the first column is accomplished. In what way will your life be better? At this point, it might be a good idea to get together with someone you trust and ask his or her help in completing the second column. Naturally, you would help that person fill his second column, too.

The next step is to look at the resolutions you value the most, as well as the resolutions that would not be a total loss if they weren't put into action.

In the third column, renumber your resolutions. Rank them until you have identified the five most valued resolutions.

Now intently look at these five resolutions. Ask yourself, as you read each one, "Is this a pie-in-the-sky that will never come true?"

Finally, circle the resolutions—one, two, or five—that are *really* achievable.

---

*Simon, S. B. *Meeting Yourself Halfway*. Niles, IL: Argus Communications, 1974. For information about current Values Realization materials and a schedule of nationwide training workshops, contact Sidney B. Simon, Old Mountain Road, Hadley, MA 01035.

Table 6. Case Study: Teacher's Watch Disappears.*

Andy Law was just reaching into an aquarium in which he kept aquatic worms when someone knocked on his door. He went to answer the knock, stepped outside to talk with the vice-principal who needed to ask him something and came back into the room within one minute. Returning to the aquarium, he noticed that his new digital watch, which he had set down on the table on which the aquarium was resting, was missing.

Andy turned to the class and said, "Okay, guys, a joke is a joke, but I want my watch back. My wife gave it to me as an engagement gift. She'll kill me if I lose it. I'm going down to the teachers' lounge to drink one bottle of soda. Then I am coming back. I want that watch on my desk when I get here. See ya."

Andy did as he said, and when he returned to the room, his watch was on his desk. He said, "Thanks, guys," stuck the watch in his pocket, and returned to the aquarium.

Questions for Thought and Discussion
1. What did Andy do after his watch was returned that would have prevented the problem in the first place?
2. Do you think that Andy handled this situation in the best way possible? How else might he have handled it? What might the results have been?
3. If Andy's school had an ironclad rule that teachers may not leave classes unattended, how might Andy have handled the situation without maximizing it?
4. Andy gambled and won. But suppose he had returned to the classroom to find that his watch had not been returned? How might he have proceeded then, and with what anticipated results?
5. Do you think that Andy made a mistake in not discussing the situation with his students after he got his watch back? Should anyone have been punished? Discuss fully.
6. Do you think that Andy's telling the students where he got his watch increased the possibility of its being returned?

Projects
1. What is your school's policy about classroom theft? If a theft is reported to the office, must it be in writing? Must the police be involved?
2. If you have insurance on your household goods, you may be covered against a loss of this sort under the "Mysterious Disappearance" clause which some policies contain. Check to see whether your insurance includes this coverage, see what the provisions of the coverage are, and, if you find that you are not covered, check with your insurance agent to see how you might receive such coverage.

---

*Krejewski, R. J., and Shuman, R. B. *The Beginning Teacher: a Practical Guide to Problem Solving.* Washington, DC: National Education Association, 1979.

Table 7. Self-evaluation of teaching.

Key: Place an X anywhere on the line; your marks need not be directly above a number. The following key shall be used:

1—Very dissatisfied with this.
2 —A problem, needs considerable improvement.

3—Acceptable but should improve.
4—Good, some room for improvement.
5—Very satisfied with this.

Personal Qualities

_____ Clarity
1 2 3 4 5

_____ Awareness of own
1 2 3 4 5 values, attitudes, and
feelings.

_____ Enthusiasm
1 2 3 4 5

_____ Awareness of others'
1 2 3 4 5 values, attitudes, and
               feelings.

_____ Self-confidence
1 2 3 4 5

_____ Acceptance of others.
1 2 3 4 5

Knowledges and Understanding

Knowledge of content areas:

Understanding of these teaching methods:

_____ Games and Sports
1 2 3 4 5

_____ Direct Instruction
1 2 3 4 5

_____ Gymnastics
1 2 3 4 5

_____ Problem-solving
1 2 3 4 5

_____ Dance
1 2 3 4 5

_____ Individualized Instruc-
1 2 3 4 5 tion

_____ Movement Principles
1 2 3 4 5

Instructional Competencies—Planning

_____ Selects appropriate
1 2 3 4 5 content.

_____ Provides sufficient par-
1 2 3 4 5 ticipation for all.

_____ Provides variety
1 2 3 4 5 within lesson.

_____ Structures effective
1 2 3 4 5 practice situations.

_____ Organizes efficiently.
1 2 3 4 5

_____ Plans for performance
1 2 3 4 5 feedback to students.

Instructional Competencies—Interactive

_____ Deals effectively with
1 2 3 4 5 disruptive behavior.

_____ Provides verbal feed-
1 2 3 4 5 back to students.

_____ Modifies plans when
1 2 3 4 5 appropriate.

_____ Uses student ideas.
1 2 3 4 5

Instructional Competencies—Evaluative

_____ Continually assesses
1 2 3 4 5 growth of individual
               students.

_____ Encourages students to
1 2 3 4 5 evaluate themselves.

_____ Thoughtfully evalu-
1 2 3 4 5 ates own planning
               and behavior after
               each lesson.

Comments and Plans for Improvement:

Table 8. Analysis of teaching.*

Definitions, Procedures, and Ground Rules for Coding Student Time in Activities

Category Definitions

1. *Performs motor activity:* Actively engages in motor task normally considered to be the subject matter of physical education, including playing game or sport, practicing skill, performing exercise or calisthenics, and exploring solutions to movement problems.
2. *Receives information:* Listens to teacher or other student; attends to demonstration, audiovisual aid, or written material.
3. *Gives information or assists:* Talks to other students or teacher (includes asking questions); demonstrates, manually assists, or spots for others.
4. *Waits:* Engages in "holding" behavior, e.g., waiting his turn, waiting for game to begin, etc. Is not performing motor activity or giving or receiving information.
5. *Relocates:* Moves from one place to another, such as walking from one activity area to another, or walking to get in line. Is not giving or receiving information.
6. *Other:* Engages in activity other than those mentioned above, such as obtaining equipment, getting drink of water, tying shoes, etc.

Coding Procedures

1. Select a target student.
2. Select an appropriate starting point. Code the student's behavior for 3 minutes; then rest for 3 minutes; then code for 3 minutes; and so on.
3. Code behavior at the end of every 5-second interval by placing a check in the category that *best describes* the type of behavior the student engaged in during that interval.
4. At the end of each 3-minute interval use the "notations" column to record any comments that will help you to recollect specific events in the coding segment.
5. At the conclusion of the period, total the checks in each column and calculate the percentage of time spent in each type of activity. Make appropriate entries under Summary Comments and Evaluation.

Special Ground Rules

1. If two or more types of behavior occur during an interval, code the type of behavior that consumed the greater portion of the interval. For example, if the student "waited" for 2 seconds and practiced for 3 seconds, code as "performed motor activity."
2. If two types of behavior occur *simultaneously* for the major portion of an interval (which sometimes happens when students receive information while they are performing a motor activity), code both behaviors.
3. Consider the student to be performing a motor activity when he or she is executing a movement, or in a "ready position," or completing a follow-through; or if a game is being played, consider the student to be performing when "time is in" for him or her.

---

*Anderson, W. G. *Analysis of Teaching Physical Education.* St. Louis, MO: C. V. Mosby, 1980.

create such an environment for yourself? At first your new job will provide plenty of challenge for you. But as your work becomes more routine, you may need to seek ways to enhance your growth, to stay alive and interested in your work.

One of the ways to enhance professional growth is to establish a support system among colleagues in the school. Teachers generally work in isolation. They rarely observe each other teach and often do not discuss their work with one another. In interviewing successful experienced teachers, Earls[5] found that they recommended observation of other teachers and programs and sharing sessions with colleagues as effective ways to sustain interest and improve teaching effectiveness. It is important to have a friend who also teaches who can be your confidant so that gripes, fears, frustrations, or inadequacies can surface and not be threatening to your career. Choose someone you can relate to and trust, possibly someone who is experienced and "knows the ropes."

In some cases the school may provide a mechanism for discussions with colleagues. Inservice sessions or department meetings may address teaching concerns. Some schools have a "buddy" system in which a new teacher is assigned an experienced teacher who provides advice and assistance. However, in many cases no formal support system exists. You may have to take the initiative by seeking out others to discuss your experiences and concerns. Some teachers may be reluctant to discuss educational issues. At first you may want to limit yourself to seeking advice rather than debating various points of view. Eventually a more open exchange of ideas may be possible. If there are several beginning teachers in your school, you might consider starting a discussion group to help each other in handling problems and issues. Discussing actual problems or case studies such as the one presented in Table 6 may help you to decide how to react in similar circumstances.

You may find that one of your experienced colleagues emerges as your mentor. A mentor can serve as a career model and can guide and support you as you learn to be an effective teacher. Such a relationship requires considerable trust and loyalty. Although the buddy system may encourage such mentoring, one of the risks may be that the assigned "buddy" may be expected by the administration to evaluate as well as help the new teacher. Such a dual role can be a threat to you and diminish the effectiveness of the mentoring system.

In addition to support from colleagues within the school, you may need to establish a network of contacts with other professionals in the field. Professional organizations provide one source of outside contact. Maintaining communication with the university from which you graduated or entering a graduate program are other alternatives. Attending conferences and workshops and reading professional journals can also be helpful. While outside professional contacts lack the intimacy and common experience characteristic of support groups within the school, they are a source of new ideas which can dispel complacency and provide stimulus for growth.

Another strategy for continued professional development is to vary your instructional activities. As a beginning teacher, you have probably focused upon mastery of a particular teaching style that feels comfortable to you. Eventually you will discover that doing things the same way may not always be effective

---

[5]Earls, N. F. "How Teachers Avoid Burnout." *Journal of Physical Education, Recreation and Dance 52* (9): 41–3.

and can lead to boredom. Experimenting with your own teaching can keep your work more interesting and can help you to improve your teaching skills.

One approach to this process is to analyze the way you are presently teaching and determine what changes you think might be desirable. A self-evaluation of teaching is described in Table 7. Completing such an evaluation might help you set goals for professional growth. Your self-evaluation should be based upon a careful analysis of your teaching. Often teachers are unaware of some aspects of their teaching behaviors. Several techniques for analysis of teaching are described in the recommended readings by Anderson (1980) and Siedentop (1982). An example of one such activity is described in Table 8. You may wish to further your analysis by videotaping or audiotaping your teaching, or by working with a colleague who could observe your classes. Student evaluations and comments might also provide useful information. The systematic analysis process involves periodic information gathering interspersed with goal-setting and efforts to change specific aspects of teaching behavior.

Another approach to the improvement of teaching is to conduct mini-experiments in which you try different ways of teaching the same thing. What would happen if you taught tennis skills in a different order in one of your classes? Could you use problem-solving to teach strategy in soccer? Do students prefer running or rope jumping as a means of attaining aerobic fitness? Will students who experience reciprocal teaching in which they assist another student become more helpful in other settings? Your mini-experiments will have some limitations; what works in one situation might not work in other circumstances. However, such examination of alternatives can be a valuable way to improve your teaching.

Another approach to keeping your teaching interesting is to get involved in a special program. You might start a class for obese children or a running club or fitness program for the faculty. Doing something special can be a very satisfying experience. Feelings of satisfaction and success in your work can contribute to your self-esteem and to your continued commitment to a teaching career.[6]

Your approach to your work is important to your personal and professional development but so is your life outside of school. Teaching is an emotionally-and physically-demanding occupation. Maintaining one's health and enthusiasm requires time away from the job. What are your personal interests and hobbies unrelated to teaching? Do you find time to pursue them? Devoting time to personal interests can provide relaxation and diversion from your work as well as stimulus for growth. This "caring for yourself" also indicates a healthy self-esteem.

Summer vacations provide an excellent opportunity to pursue personal growth activities. Summer activities which are very different from your teaching and coaching responsibilities may be an effective way to avoid burnout.[7] Travel, graduate school, or a summer job unrelated to teaching may help you to be a more interesting and interested person when you return to school in the fall.

---

[6]Harootunian, B., and Yarger, G. P. *Teachers Conceptions of Their Own Success.* Washington, DC: ERIC Clearinghouse on Teacher Education, 1981.
[7]Earls, 1981.

Being a Professional

Educators generally assume that teaching is a profession much like law and medicine. Professionals have unique expertise and knowledge which permits them to perform a socially valuable service to other people. Professionals have the autonomy to make professional judgments and the responsibility for performing that service ethically and well. Because of their qualifications, professionals are granted an exclusive right to practice and are afforded high status in society. Members of the profession establish and enforce standards of quality for their work.

Is teaching a profession? In contrast to doctors and lawyers, teachers are employees of a large bureaucratic organization which may limit their professional autonomy. Some people have questioned the extent to which teachers possess unique expertise and knowledge. Many people believe that any educated adult can teach. For this reason, teaching sometimes has been called a semi-profession and teachers continue their struggle for professional recognition and rewards.[8] Each of you will become part of that struggle. As you seek more autonomy or higher status, you will be saying to the public "I have unique expertise and can provide a valuable service to your children."

What is it that you as a physical educator can do that is unique? What can you do that cannot be done by the Little League coach or the former varsity tennis player who teaches tennis at the park? Why should the school pay you a professional salary to supervise the physical activity of students?

The evidence of your professionalism will rest primarily upon the quality of the program you conduct. Your instruction will reflect your unique expert knowledge about student development, physical education subject matter, and instructional techniques. The program will provide a valuable service to all students and not just to the highly skilled athlete. As a professional, you will assume personal responsibility for the quality of your services regardless of whether the organization encourages or rewards such quality.

Maintaining professional standards while surviving within the bureaucracy of the school system is not easy. It requires personal strength and continuous growth and renewal. The rewards of a professional career are a sense of satisfaction and accomplishment that are sometimes difficult to see. The student who comes back after graduation to say, "you made a difference," can make your efforts seem worthwhile. Aiming toward continuous personal and professional growth enables teaching to be all that it can and should be.

Recommended Readings

Anderson, W. G. *Analysis of Teaching Physical Education*. St. Louis, MO: C. V. Mosby, 1980.

Krejewski, R. J., and Shuman, R. B. *The Beginning Teacher: a Practical Guide to Problem Solving*. Washington, DC: National Education Assocation, 1979.

Lawson, H. A., and Placek, J. H. *Physical Education in the Secondary Schools*. Boston, MA: Allyn and Bacon, 1981, pp. 4–26.

Ryan, K. et al. *Biting the Apple: Accounts of First Year Teachers*. New York: Longman, Inc., 1980.

Siedentop, D. *Developing Teaching Skills in Physical Education*. 2d ed. Palo Alto, CA: Mayfield Publishing, 1982.

---

[8]Etzioni, A., ed. *The Semi-professions and Their Organization: Teachers, Nurses and Social Workers*. New York: Free Press, 1969.